Career Networking

*The **Insider Guides** is a dynamic series of books which together form the ultimate career companion.*

Whether looking for that first job, or hoping to develop your current career, each title in the series offers practical advice and real-life insights to put you on the inside track to success.

Other titles in the series:

Job Search
Brian Sutton

Interviews & Assessments
Brian Sutton

Career Networking

Networking for career and job success

by

Brian Sutton

First published in 2000 by
The Industrial Society
Robert Hyde House
48 Bryanston Square
London W1H 2EA

© Brian Sutton 2000

ISBN 1 85835 825 6

British Library Cataloguing-in-Publication Data.
A catalogue record for this book is available from
the British Library.

Typeset by: The Midlands Book Typesetting Company
Printed by: Cromwell Press
Cover by: Sign Design
Cover image by: Andrew Hall/Tony Stone Images

The Industrial Society is a Registered Charity No. 290003

CONTENTS

ACKNOWLEDGEMENTS

It is a pleasure to acknowledge the help I have received from all those who have provided me with views and opinions quoted in this book. To my editor, Susannah Lear, I owe a special debt of gratitude for offering me the opportunity to write all three books in this important career series. Last, but by no means least, I am grateful to my wife Jacquey for her distinctive blend of encouragement and support.

INTRODUCTION

Management has always had its share of jargon. We can all think of examples, many of which are no longer in fashion. However, networking is one of those words which has been around for a long time, and we seem to hear it more often these days. What exactly, then, is networking? As the word indicates, networking is the exchange of information or services within a network or chain of interconnected people. An easy way of understanding what happens within a personal network is to compare it with the world's largest computer network known as the Internet. In this system, millions of computers are connected so that they can share information. In personal networks, people are connected or linked together so that they can share information.

During the research for this book, I very quickly realised that in the world of work people have their own ideas about the meaning of networking. Here's a selection of their views:

'It's helping people to achieve their career goals.'
Consultant – search and selection company

'It's a tactic for establishing and developing worthwhile business contacts.'
Managing director – engineering company

'It's a great way of sharing ideas with people in the same field of work.'
Training manager – retailing company

'It's the best way of hearing about IT vacancies.'
Systems development specialist – computer manufacturer

'It's something I've been doing as a natural part of my job.'
Operations supervisor – electronics manufacturer

What all these views have in common is the idea of linking up or making connections with other people. One connection leads to another connection, which leads to yet more, and so on. This is what networking is all about. The other message that comes across from these views is that it's not simply about making connections with *anybody*. In fact, quite the opposite is true. It's about making connections with appropriate and useful people, building up a community of contacts across personal, social, business and professional networks. The conclusion to draw from this is that all those within the network hope to get something out of it.

My research revealed that effective networking is seen as vital if you want to succeed in the world of work. Some people went so far as to say that without it opportunities for development and advancement would be limited and your career would stagnate.

As you may now have gathered, networking is not a new technique. Most of us have probably practised it without ever giving it that label. Humans are highly social creatures, and those who enjoy interacting with others will find networking a truly beneficial experience. If you've ever made contact with buyers, organised a social or sporting event or attended a meeting of your local Chamber of Commerce, you have networked. Building and managing your networks can make the difference for you, both personally and professionally, and help you with career change, career development and job search.

Networking can be both enjoyable and rewarding, and it's never too early or too late to begin developing and making the most of your networking skills.

This book is the second in a series of *Insider Guides* for all those who want to achieve career and job-search success in a changing workplace. The first book in this series, *Job Search*, contains all the advice you'll need to locate vacancies and secure interviews. The third book follows close upon the heels of *Career Networking* and is entitled *Interviews & Assessments*.

The first chapter of this book demystifies the technique

of networking and answers the question 'Why is networking so important?' It considers the changing world of work and explains how learning to adapt can prove to be a valuable asset. *Accept responsibility for your own career development* is the strong message to be found in this chapter, and how creating networks is the key to successful career development.

You need to exploit networking to the full and Chapter 2 gives advice on how to build and develop networks. Choosing your contacts carefully, organising yourself and expanding your network are all essential requirements.

Chapter 3 concentrates on the importance of acquiring networking skills. You will discover how to improve your personal skills, and make a success of networking. You will read about the importance of effective communication, verbal and non-verbal methods of gaining co-operation and how to overcome shyness.

Chapter 4 explains why using networking to access the hidden recruitment market should be a vital part of your career change or job-search strategy. Techniques for arranging networking meetings and sample networking letters can all be found in this chapter, together with advice on how best to conduct yourself when meeting contacts you know personally, contacts to whom you are referred and contacts in the recruitment business.

Chapter 5 shows you how networking can be used to target specific employers. The importance of focused research is explained. Again, examples of networking letters are included, together with advice on how best to conduct yourself when meeting targeted employers.

Chapter 6 examines how networking can help you to protect your career, by taking responsibility for your continuing education and building up your visibility.

Chapter 7 concludes with a brief summary of the essential features and benefits of networking.

With checklists, case studies, quotes from insiders and 'myth busters' that challenge commonly held beliefs, *Career Networking* should provide all the practical help and support you need. Read in conjunction with the other

two books in this series, *Job Search* and *Interviews &
Assessments*, you will have the complete guide to career and
job-search success.

Why networking skills are important

THE CHANGING NATURE OF CAREERS

Because the fabric and character of careers are being affected by changes taking place in the world of work, the subject is an important issue for career changers and job searchers. Employees in organisations large and small can confirm that change is ever-present. Employers reacted to falls in consumer demand during the recession, and have had to respond positively to increased competition whilst improving the quality and reliability of their products and services. Also, the pace of technological change continues to have a major effect on many organisations and occupations. These changes have not been limited to the UK, which strongly suggests that we are entering a new age where work is going global.

Many employers recognise that in order to survive they must restructure, take over other businesses, downsize, outsource, merge and subcontract. Failure to do so will guarantee a bleak future. Set against this background of unprecedented change, what is the future for careers?

From early childhood, we're taught to equate progress with promotions, and many people have grown up in a world where they have been encouraged to think of their career in these terms. Gone are the days when working for one or perhaps two employers during a lifetime was the accepted career path, and frequent changes of employer were seen as a sign of instability. Times have certainly changed, because fewer and fewer organisations now offer this traditional type of career. In fact, those who still cling to the idea of staying with one employer for life may well be damaging their career development. Today, lifetime careers in one organisation are being replaced by multiple careers in several. Even within the same organisation, an employee can have many roles. Consequently, developing your key transferable skills will greatly improve your employability and enable you to cope with the likelihood of changing your employer more frequently.

Just as organisations are changing in order to survive, so you, too, must learn to adapt. You can expect flexible ways of working and your responsibilities will regularly change. Aligning yourself with your employer's needs and responding quickly will greatly enhance your value to the employer.

Technology continues to have a considerable impact on jobs. For the future you'll need to understand and use new technology to a far greater extent than in the past. In fact, you will need a greater skill level than before. You can no longer afford to sit back and rely on your employer to take care of your development and training. In the new world of work, whatever your situation, whether you are just starting or midway through your career, there is one thing you can do to help your employability: take the initiative and create the opportunities to learn something new. Learning new ideas, new systems and new processes means you stay employable. Consequently, when you're faced with job search, all your training and self-development moves with you.

Adapting to these changes isn't easy. However, the good news is that the job is alive and well, so meet change with change: take control of your career, set realistic career goals, invest in your own education, accept responsibility for your own personal development and training, and develop networks.

'Promotion opportunities in this company are open to anyone who has a combination of the right technical skills plus commitment and a willingness to help drive the company forward.'
Human resource manager – computer hardware manufacturer

'Teamwork, a willingness to learn and behaving as though this was your own business are the qualities we value the most.'
Sales director – sales and marketing specialists

THE VALUE OF NETWORKING

As people advance through their careers, they often find that they need more than just technical skills to succeed. Success today depends more and more on how well we build good relationships with subordinates, peers, superiors, teams, customers, suppliers and many others.

Building relationships has always been important for managers. However, in this changing world of work, new ways of managing are required in which relationship skills are crucial. Success now depends on how well managers build and maintain their network of contacts.

The first book in this series, *Job Search*, revealed how the hidden job market (i.e. those jobs that have not been advertised) accounts for 80% of the available vacancies. However, what is of real interest is that most career specialists and outplacement consultants agree that networking is the most productive source of vacancies in the hidden job market. It's precisely because of networking's effectiveness in this area that it should lie at the heart of managing your career and your employability in the changing world of work. You may not be able to pick up the phone and speak directly to the managing director of the company you would like to work for, but one of your contacts might be able to make that call on your behalf.

Networking is not only important from a career-change or job-search point of view, but is increasingly important for doing business and at all stages of career development. In addition, because networking is about relationships, it's just as critical for your personal happiness and physical well-being.

Networks provide an entrance or doorway to:

- **Company decision-makers.** These are the people responsible for creating jobs well before a decision is taken to advertise them in the open market. They also have the authority to make offers of employment.

- **Sources of information.** We all need information in many different forms. Information enables us to work better, forecast future trends, solve problems and manage difficult situations. Networking is a well-proven method of *discovering* matters of interest from an industry, organisation and personal viewpoint. It provides knowledge, by allowing you to study and learn from successful people and businesses. In networking, people use each other to close the information gap between what they know and what they *need* to know in order to advance their careers.

- **Spheres of influence.** Networking enables you to identify key people and forge relationships, whilst improving your visibility and enhancing your reputation in the business community. It provides the opportunity to influence the opinions and attitudes of others. Networking also allows you to test your behaviour, ideas and strategies for success before risking them in the real world. The feedback, whether positive or negative, will be invaluable.

These three doorways provide an opportunity to build a well-developed network of contacts that are vital for effective self-marketing – an important strategy when considering career change or job search. Unfortunately, the value of networking is often appreciated too late; for some people this is when their career is in crisis. If your job provides you with little opportunity to meet people inside or outside your organisation, then you need to manage your time better. Without the ability to create a well-developed network of contacts, you may, for example, find it extremely difficult to recover from the shock of redundancy. Networking is a long-term strategy, so don't wait until you're desperate before developing your network; it will be too late!

As with all your training and self-development, your networks are also portable. You take your contacts with you wherever you go. Your challenge is to build the right networks. Managing your career well means building relationships that help with job search and manoeuvre you into the best position for future career moves.

MYTH BUSTER
People are not really interested in helping others

Not true! The success of networking disproves this myth. Because networking is about mutual benefit, you may have as much to offer your contacts as they can offer you. Many people are flattered to be asked for advice, and experience a genuine sense of satisfaction if they have been able to help others in their network. They know that if they should ever need help or support, it will be given without counting the cost.

NETWORKING FOR MUTUAL BENEFIT

The essence of networking is that the benefit is mutual. You must know not only the strengths of your principal contacts but their personal needs as well. Networking is not a one-way street. So, it's important to clarify both your own needs and the likely needs of your principal contacts. See what you can offer them in return for their help. This will give you a clear picture of your relationship. The rhythm of responsiveness between you and your contacts is as important in relationship-building as in a conversation. If you don't respond to friendly overtures from your contact, you'll break the rhythm. If your contacts don't respond to you, they may be unhappy about the relationship.

Because networking is about mutuality, you must be prepared to come to the aid of your contacts if they call on you for help. Just as you may need advice and guidance from them, you too must keep track of the information that could help them in their hour of need.

'When I contacted a colleague of mine for some career advice, I expected him to fight shy of getting involved because the last time we spoke was six months before. However, I was really surprised because he was so enthusiastic. I imagine this must be because he was grateful for the information I sent him to help with his degree course.'

Customer support supervisor – mobile communications industry

REMEMBER

✔ The changes that have taken place in the world of work are an important issue for career changers and job searchers.

✔ Lifetime careers in one organisation are being replaced by multiple careers in several.

✔ Developing your key transferable skills will greatly improve your employability.

✔ Learn to adapt and align yourself with your employer's needs.

✔ To help your employability, take the initiative and create the opportunities to learn something new.

✔ Invest in your own education and accept responsibility for your own personal development and training.

✔ Networking is the most productive source of vacancies in the hidden job market.

✔ A well-developed network of contacts is vital for effective self-marketing – an important strategy for career change or job search.

✔ Don't wait until you're desperate before developing your network; it will be too late!

✔ The essence of networking is mutual benefit.

From the outset, it's important to exploit the potential of networking to the full. In order to do this, you must build and develop your networks. Your task is to make principal contacts that lead to referred contacts. Principal contacts are those people you know first-hand who can help you with your career or job search. These contacts then review their own networks to find others to whom you can be referred. Hence, referred contacts are people to whom you have been directed by a principal contact.

CHOOSING PRINCIPAL CONTACTS

The first part of your networking strategy is to identify potential contacts. To begin with, you need a list of everyone you know personally. This list could be made up of the following:

- personal contacts
- social contacts
- business and professional contacts.

Personal contacts

Personal contacts are people close to you, such as relatives, friends and others, where the relationship is based on mutuality and liking and where trust is implicit in the relationship.

The first network we recognise is that of the family. Family members have a strong bonding that produces feelings of love, affection and loyalty; this means they will often work hard on your behalf. Remember too that family members have their own networks and their referrals can be highly effective.

Contact flow-chart

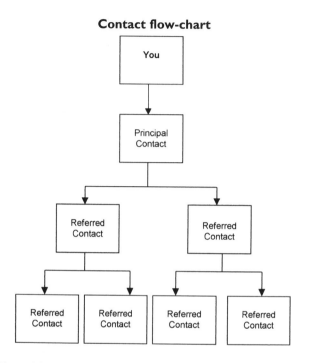

Friendships can be developed in a variety of settings – through the family, school, university or work.

Social contacts

Shared interests or hobbies bring people together to produce social networks. These are great opportunities for building contacts. Contacts in this group may at some stage transfer to your network of personal contacts as friendships develop. Here are some examples:

- sports and social clubs
- hobby and recreational clubs
- theatre and drama groups
- religious groups
- teachers/lecturers
- Territorial Army
- local political groups
- Parent Teachers Association
- study and educational classes

- charity groups
- local or parish council.

Business and professional contacts

Business and professional contacts are acquired through work and work interests. The relationship with contacts can be a formal one, as is often the case with customers, suppliers and trade associations, whilst others can be informal, as, for example, with fellow members of the Rotary Club and professional institutes. Contacts in this network can be of real value for your career development and job search, because they have access to those people responsible for creating jobs. Throughout your working day, you can tap into this network as part of your normal duties and responsibilities.

When building relationships in the workplace, it's important to understand your organisation's politics. In every company there are those you should stay well clear of and those who can be of real help. Forming a relationship with the wrong contact won't help your strategy and may well affect how others view you in the organisation. So, don't rush into making contacts in the workplace; instead, monitor the climate carefully before making any decisions.

There are many opportunities for networking outside of work, such as professional institutes and trade organisations. Some of these also conduct social events and shared meetings with other organisations.

Always keep your relationship on a professional footing until you get to know the contact well and feel you can trust them. If you let your guard down too soon, some casual remark on your part may find its way back to your employer.

> 'I worked hard at developing a good relationship with our clients. At first, the relationship was entirely professional but eventually I broke down the formal barriers. I found that you needed to adjust your style to suit the occasion.'
>
> *Claims inspector – insurance industry*

Business and professional networks are great sources of information that help you to keep up to date in your chosen profession. Many offer the possibility of finding mentors – senior people in the profession who are willing to share their experience with you and offer advice and guidance. In addition, networking will also create opportunities for you to become a mentor, which in turn helps your personal growth.

Here are some examples of contacts in this network:

- solicitor
- Rotary Club/Round Table members
- business suppliers
- current and previous employers
- recruitment consultants
- professional institutes
- consultants (general)
- business associates (past and present)
- Chamber of Commerce members
- bankers
- clients and customers
- industry events/exhibitions
- employment agencies
- training events
- trade organisations
- careers adviser
- personal accountant
- business cards collected
- journalists and reporters
- guest speakers
- stockbroker.

You may be surprised to discover how many people you *do* know. Your principal contacts and their referred contacts connect you to a large network. However, to begin with you must evaluate who would be the most valuable in assisting you with your career and job search. In order to do this you need to develop a set of criteria. For example:

- People who are approachable, supportive and easy to talk to.
- People who have knowledge of your job and the industry in which you work.
- People who understand your career needs.
- People who can offer you constructive advice and guidance.
- People with a wide-ranging network of contacts.
- People who have established successful careers.
- People with status and influence who can link up with decision-makers.
- People who have access to a network suitable for your needs.
- People who can share their network with yours.
- People you admire for their popularity and ability to make contacts.

Choosing principal contacts is never easy, but it's vital to be selective at this stage. So choose people who have strong networks of their own so that you can add as many referred contacts to your network as possible. Their role in your network is to provide a doorway to company decision-makers, sources of information and spheres of influence.

If you have problems identifying enough principal contacts, it can be helpful to consult your office diary for past appointments, company addresses, home addresses and telephone numbers, as well as directories of trade and professional associations. All of these can also help to jog your memory. If you have a partner, it's also a good idea to involve them in identifying any shared contacts. Take a clean piece of paper, and make a list of your contacts straightaway. Against each name, write down whether they are a contact from your friends, social or business and professional network.

MYTH BUSTER
Network contacts must always be company directors or senior managers

Wrong! People from all walks of life, irrespective of their seniority, can make useful contacts. Don't be too narrow in your choice of contacts; it's more important to know whether your contacts can offer you useful advice and support and if they have access to networks of their own.

NETWORKING DIRECTORY

Now that your list is complete, it's important to record information about each of your principal contacts in a standard format. Here's an example:

NETWORKING DIRECTORY

Contact's full name (and nickname):

Home address and telephone number:

Name and address of employing company:

Telephone number:

Fax number:

E-mail address:

Secretary's name and telephone extension:

Relationship with the contact:

Any other information and background on this contact:

Details of meetings with this contact:

Letters sent to contact on:

Referred to:

Address and telephone number:

Details of appointment with referred contact:

Referred to:

Address and telephone number:

Details of appointment with referred contact:

To network effectively, you must be well organised. Using this or a similar form will certainly help.

EXPANDING YOUR NETWORK

Your next step is to look carefully at your list of principal contacts and see if you can identify any gaps in your network. Do you have enough principal contacts with strong networks of their own who can assist you with your career development and job search? If the answer is 'no', then speed up the process of expanding your network by consciously making new contacts.

In order to determine how effective you are at building relationships, ask yourself the following questions:

- Do you make opportunities to meet new people?
- Do you regularly attend meetings at work or socially?
- Are you a member of any clubs or associations?
- Do you introduce yourself to speakers at training courses, conferences and dinners?
- Have your contacts grown in number over the last few years?
- Do you share information with other people?
- Do you talk to your peers in other companies?
- Do you work at establishing a close connection with customers?
- If you needed urgent help with your career, do you know people who would be prepared to help?
- Are you generally well informed and up to date with information affecting the company and industry within which you work?

If you have answered 'no' to any of these questions, try to identify what is preventing you from building relationships. If it's an inability to market yourself properly, then the next chapter, 'Essential skills for networking', will help.

～MYTH BUSTER～
Network contacts have to be people you know well

Wrong! You have to work at building relationships with people who are complete strangers. This means finding opportunities to meet people in a range of different settings; taking the initiative and finding something in common that allows the relationship to develop.

There are many ways of meeting new people, and although they won't all present opportunities for developing contacts, be prepared to keep an open mind.

'When I meet people in a social setting I admit to finding it difficult to network. After all, it's so easy to put people off by talking "shop". I find the best way of handling this is to ask the question "How's the job going?" – this usually prompts the contact to do most of the talking.'

Personnel officer – pharmaceuticals industry

Mobility can help with network-building. It keeps you in the swim of things and provides new venues, new places and people, and new opportunities to make contacts. Why not volunteer to take on a temporary assignment in another part of the company, join new committees and teams or participate in company social events?

If you meet someone with whom you have something in common and who you think would make a good principal contact, you may have to take the initiative and make the first move. Make a point of swapping business cards and, if possible, try to obtain the name of their secretary and their home telephone number. Afterwards, record all this information on a network directory form or in your PC software. When you next get in touch, don't let them think that you want something for nothing: for example, sending them some of your company brochures.

This isn't the way to ensure a long-term relationship. However, don't let the opportunity pass without arranging another meeting, perhaps at a similar venue or as a guest over a meal in your office restaurant. This is an important way of cementing your relationship and jointly recognising how you can be of help to each other. Following this second meeting, send your contact a short letter. This creates a good impression and helps to 'fix' the relationship in your contact's memory. Here are several examples of this type of letter:

Springfield Engineering Co. Ltd
Unit 24, Harley Industrial Estate, Birmingham QQ8 2TT
Telephone: 0121 123 4567

Mr David Smith
Contracts Manager
GWA Canning Co. Ltd
Swan Lane
Birmingham XY9 ZA2

19 July 2000

Dear David

It was good to meet up with you again over lunch in Springfield's restaurant. I hope the food was to your liking!

As you know, I've been asked to make a short presentation at our institute meeting during September. As both GWA Canning and Springfield Engineering are so strongly linked in the market-place, we agreed it would be a good idea to spend approximately ten minutes each talking about our respective companies. I hope that we can raise the awareness of our members to the issues facing the industry. Can I suggest that we meet up at 7.45pm on 14 September just to get our act together before the meeting starts? If this is a problem, do give me a call.

My best wishes to you and your family.

Malcolm Jennings
Malcolm Jennings

Kingsway Computer Software Co. Ltd
33 The Commercial Centre, Macclesfield MW8 7EE
Telephone: 01625 910011

Mrs Margaret Vickers
Human Resources Manager
Broadhead Insurance Co. Ltd
Claypole Drive
Macclesfield MW9 6RR

26 July 2000

Dear Margaret

Thank you for coming to address our local business meeting. I found your choice of subject very interesting.

I suggested that we should meet up again so that I can give you some further background to the local business group. Would you be able to meet me for lunch next Friday 30 July? If you can, call into my office first at 12.15pm. The restaurant is only a short walk away. I'll arrange a parking space for you in the company car park. Please give me a call to confirm your availability.

Kind regards

Frank Owen
Frank Owen

HOLDING ON TO YOUR EXISTING CONTACTS

Introducing new contacts to fill the gaps in your network is essential, but so is holding on to your existing contacts. Keeping in touch is the key to good networking, so plan and diary when you intend to phone them. Try to find some information that your contact will be interested in, and always make sure you ask about themselves and their families. If you can tie these calls into a special occasion, such as a birthday or wedding anniversary, so much the better. It's up to you to determine how often you call your contacts. You may need to call some more frequently than others. One note of warning – don't over-communicate, as this can be irritating; conversely, don't let your contacts go cold through lack of communication.

Whilst the telephone is a good way of keeping in touch, it's always best to meet your contacts in person. Find reasons to meet up for the occasional drink after work or invite a contact over for a meal in the company restaurant. If you hear about a promotion or transfer, send them a letter and follow this up with a phone call. If you've selected the right people as contacts, and put enough effort into networking, your contacts will also keep in touch with you.

Every time you meet someone new, you have expanded your network, so try to keep in networking mode. Remember to add their details to your network directory: this way you will always keep track of your contacts and have useful information at your fingertips.

NETWORKING PROTOCOL

Protocol is important in networking. Follow these rules if you want to make the most of your networking opportunities:

- Never be afraid to ask your contacts for help, advice and support. There's little point in building networks if you don't make use of them.
- Whilst the essence of networking is mutual benefit, don't do too much for your contacts before you ask them to do something in return. Otherwise, this might imply that your contacts have nothing to offer, and they may hesitate to ask again.
- Helping those in your network is not about *quid pro quo*. Never seriously suggest to your contacts they 'they owe you one': this will damage your reputation in the network and may lead to a loss of principal contacts. Remember when giving that you'll benefit at some later stage.
- Don't focus on any one contact at the expense of others in your network. Apart from the risk of becoming over-reliant on them, you may lose others because of lack of communication.

- Don't share confidential information that you have received from one of your contacts with anyone else. If your contact finds out, you'll lose their trust.
- Be natural with your contacts and don't oversell.
- Don't show off in front of your contacts. They'll almost certainly dislike you for it.
- Always be considerate with your requests for help and support. Don't put your contacts under pressure. Make sure you respect their wishes, and contact them at home or at the office, whichever they prefer.
- When someone helps you, always say 'thank you', either by phoning your contact or writing them a short letter.
- Always keep your promises. If you agree to do something for someone, don't let them down; they won't forget. Keeping your promises will build the trust you need.
- Don't whinge, complain or gossip to people in your network.
- Always send thank-you letters promptly. This builds confidence and mutual trust.

'Sending a thank-you letter to your contacts is an important courtesy. On the few occasions I've helped someone and not received a letter, I was unimpressed.'
Managing director – electrical wholesalers industry

AVOIDING PROBLEMS

From time to time, you should examine your networks to ensure that they are still of value to you. If the relationship with one of your contacts is not yielding results, is this due to a change in their circumstances or because of neglect on your part? It may be that a brief meeting is all that's needed to get the relationship back on line. Whatever the reason, don't simply allow things to get worse. Make the effort and get in touch.

WOMEN AND NETWORKING

Whilst recognising the importance of networking skills for job search, some women may find it uncomfortable and difficult to make any real progress with networking in what some would describe as a man's world. To overcome this problem, a number of networking organisations have been formed for women and information about these can be found on the Internet. Website addresses for these organisations can be found in the resource directory at the back of this book.

Case Study

It pays to be organised

Pam was a personal assistant to the managing director of a large car-hire company and worked at their head office. The company decided it should relocate its head office, and although Pam was offered the opportunity to relocate with them, she decided not to do so because she would be moving away from her family and her friends.

During her notice period, Pam read about job search and, because she had so many friends and contacts, she decided networking would be a good way of finding her next job.

Six weeks later Pam began to run into problems. Whilst she had made good progress in talking to a number of contacts, she had upset several people by not keeping in touch and failing to record the outcome of networking meetings. Pam readily admitted that whilst she was good at organising things at work, she didn't have the same grip on things in her personal life.

Pam spent the next few days listing the names and personal details of her contacts and the outcome of her networking meetings. When this was completed she felt much more confident in dealing with her contacts.

REMEMBER

✔ Principal contacts are those people you know first-hand who can provide a doorway to company decision-makers, sources of information and spheres of influence. Referred contacts are people to whom you have been directed by a principal contact.

✔ List your principal contacts from the following groups:

- Personal contacts – these are people close to you such as relatives and friends.
- Social contacts – people with whom you share interests or hobbies.
- Business and professional contacts – these are acquired through work and work interests.

✔ Evaluate who on your list of contacts will be the most valuable in helping you with your career and job search.

✔ Use a network directory to record information about your contacts.

✔ Identify any gaps in your networks.

✔ Cultivate contacts by meeting people in different settings.

✔ Create a good impression by sending your contacts a letter after your meeting.

✔ Don't neglect your existing contacts.

It doesn't matter how many contacts you have in your networks if you don't have the skills necessary to obtain their help and support. Without these you may lose your existing contacts and find it extremely difficult to establish new ones. This chapter describes the skills you'll need for effective networking.

COMMUNICATION

Networking is about communication, and the best networkers are outstanding communicators. Effective communication should always be a two-way process. However, simply attaching importance to verbal and written communication is not enough. Good networkers are also excellent listeners, because they know it's not so much what people say as what they mean.

You need communication skills to share ideas and experiences, to find out about things that interest you and to explain to people what you want.

Good communication enables you to make yourself known to potential contacts, to build friendships and to forge effective relationships. Being a good communicator is about sending and receiving messages, listening and understanding in the context of an open supportive relationship. Networking is built on open supportive relationships. You must therefore be willing to give and take feedback and to show a respect for the needs and interests of your contacts.

To develop open supportive relationships you need the following qualities:

- *Empathy* – taking a genuine interest in others and seeing the world from the other person's point of view.
- *Unqualified respect* – although the behaviour of your contacts may not always be to your liking, this mustn't interfere with your relationship.
- *Integrity* – always saying what you mean and meaning what you say.
- *Acceptance* – accepting people for what they are and not as you would like them to be.

Networkers who possess these qualities will find their communication the most rewarding.

SELF-ESTEEM

A lack of self-esteem or belief in yourself can hinder your ability to communicate effectively. Self-esteem is linked to your self-perception: that is, how you see yourself rather than how others see you or how you'd like to be. A poor self-perception may affect your self-esteem at a very deep level and can be a crippling handicap.

It's not unusual to feel we're not as good or as capable as those around us. We know that comparing ourselves with someone who may be better qualified or more skilful can seriously damage our self-confidence. To be committed, indeed to be successful at anything, you have to believe you can do it. Employers search for this as much as any other job qualification. People who lack self-esteem, although they may say all the right things, often have a question mark in their voices.

In networking, your self-perception determines how you value yourself and what you have to say. If you don't think what you have to say is worthwhile, it can seriously affect your ability to form relationships. A person with low self-esteem often feels inferior and lacks confidence. Consequently, they may have difficulty in talking to other people, voicing ideas and expressing feelings.

Throughout life, you may have received messages that damaged your self-esteem. As a result, you gradually lose contact with your abilities, as you try to live up to other people's expectations rather than your own. For some people, this has meant entering a career of their parent's choosing instead of deciding for themselves.

Transferable skills

The good news is that you can improve your self-esteem by changing your self-perception. You are who you are, so set out to make the most of your individuality. Start by focusing on your strengths and not your weaknesses. If you have a copy of *Job Search* (the first book in this series), you'll have undertaken the self-assessment exercises, including the identification of achievements. This work would have clearly demonstrated that you have transferable skills, personal strengths and values. By concentrating on these and not your weaknesses you're accentuating the positive and eliminating the negative.

Transferable skills are those you acquire throughout life, at university, as you move from job to job, at home, or from undertaking voluntary, charitable or sporting activities. They can be divided into the following five groups:

- people skills
- reasoning and judging skills
- co-ordinating skills
- information skills and
- originating skills.

If you've not already done so, list your own transferable skills under each group, and be sure to rank them so that you're clear about which skills are your strongest assets. If you need any help with this exercise, you'll find a list of transferable skills in the skills guide at the back of this book.

Recognising and understanding your personal strengths will support the transferable skills you've identified. Begin the process by looking for evidence of achievements at work, university or college and home. Next, list the strengths you possess that have played a role in these achievements. Again, if you need any help with this exercise, consult the list of personal strengths in the skills guide on p.89.

Achievements are tasks that you've accomplished successfully through effort, practice or perseverance, using your skills and personal strengths. To prepare your list of achievements, examine your employment history, concentrating on what is most recent. Next, refer to your list of skills and personal strengths. Think carefully about each job and pick out anything significant or of particular interest.

Carrying out these exercises will build your self-esteem. Remember, negative thoughts will hold you back, so why not change them? Respond differently, and focus on positive action and reaction. Start appreciating yourself, and take pride in your accomplishments and achievements, no matter how small.

'Research shows that people like people who have a sense of humour. Having a sense of humour doesn't mean you have to tell jokes, but perhaps having a wry way of looking at the world and yourself can help.'

Headhunter

WHY LISTENING IS SO IMPORTANT

Most of us aren't good listeners. Listening is a very complex process as well as a learned skill that requires conscious effort. Very few of us have been taught effective listening skills, and yet listening affects the quality of the relationships we have with people, whether they are network contacts, friends or family members. Here are some examples of poor listening habits:

- Not paying enough attention to what the speaker is saying.
- Often easily distracted.
- Interrupting the speaker.
- Hearing what you expect to hear and not the true meaning behind the words.

- Making quick judgements about what has been said.
- Thinking about our response before the speaker has finished talking.

Listening is not just hearing; it's understanding what the speaker means to communicate. An important skill for networking is 'showing' your contacts that you *are* listening. This is all part of building effective relationships. Here are some tips to help you convey this:

- Make sure you've allocated enough time for the meeting.
- If you're seated, adopt an open posture facing the speaker.
- You have two ears and one mouth – use them in that ratio!
- Take notes, but always ask for permission to do so first.
- Listen with an open mind.
- Look at the speaker, maintain eye contact, but don't stare.
- Give the speaker time and space.
- Don't finish the other person's sentences – be patient and let them end the sentence themselves.
- Don't jump to conclusions and assume you know what the speaker is going to say.
- Encourage the speaker to continue with short statements such as 'I understand', 'Of course', 'I see'.
- The speaker needs to feel understood, so check your understanding by summarising what they have said, using their own words.
- Don't be influenced by first impressions. This may mean that you concentrate only on what is said that confirms these impressions.
- Ask questions. If you don't understand something, ask questions for clarification.
- Listen for what isn't being said.
- Listen for the ideas behind the facts. Some people don't give out information easily and you may need to ask questions for clarification.

- Pause before replying. Taking a small breath before responding shows that you're giving some consideration to your answer. It also allows the other person time to expand on the information they've already given you. This additional information may prove to be very useful.

'My advice is to be like a chameleon in adjusting your behaviour to match your contact's styles, particularly on your first meeting. What you're doing is making your contact feel more comfortable and this is more likely to generate a second meeting.'

Headhunter

PREPARING TO COMMUNICATE

Because communication is the key to successful networking, you should always prepare what you want to say before meeting your contacts. Have a clear-cut objective for the meeting so that you keep on track. Decide in advance what outcome you want from the meeting, and when would be the best time and place to meet, making sure you have all the information on the contact that you need.

SECURING CO-OPERATION

For your networks to work effectively, you need the co-operation of your contacts. There are a variety of methods, both verbal and non-verbal, you can use to secure this co-operation. With the verbal method, your approach can be passive, aggressive, indirect or assertive.

Verbal methods of securing co-operation

The passive approach
Those who are passive often believe that what happens to them is someone else's fault and not their own. They never take control of their own destiny and regularly allow others to take decisions for them. Frightened of being noticed, the passive person will seldom ask their contacts for anything. They rarely show their feelings even when

they disapprove. As a result, others either assume they approve or feel that it's unnecessary to take their feelings or opinions into account. Convinced that they have nothing to give to networking, passive people often wait for contacts to come to them rather than taking the initiative.

The aggressive approach
An aggressive person is the direct opposite of the passive type. These people want to dominate others and take control of situations before they themselves are controlled. They demand that their priorities be met, often at the expense of others and without taking their views into account. Aggressive people are readily critical; they overreact, are notorious for launching verbal attacks and often hurt others without feeling remorse. They rarely get co-operation from their peers, and subordinate staff lack motivation and feel demeaned. This type of behaviour is often adopted by people to cover up their own shortcomings and feelings of inadequacy. As networkers, they have little to offer, because they always take without giving back in return.

The indirect approach
A person using the indirect approach tries to obtain co-operation from others with insincere flattery and a thin veneer of friendliness. They are hypocritical and give superficial compliments simply to get their own way. Conversely, this type of person uses sarcasm and non-verbal indirect criticisms so that everyone except the object of their criticism can see what they're doing. In networking, this type of person tries to manipulate their contacts, and in the short term may even succeed. However, people soon become distrustful and sever the link.

The assertive approach
Assertive behaviour is the most effective method to use if you want to get the co-operation of your contacts. Being assertive means letting your contacts know what your

wants and needs are whilst also taking their views and opinions into account. Be honest with them so that they understand how important this is to you.

Assertiveness comes naturally when you feel good about yourself and take pride in your accomplishments and achievements. You'll find that your contacts are more likely to respect you, and feel respected by you, when you're assertive. Stating clearly what you want will enable you to get and keep your contact's attention.

An assertive person is confident, aware of their feelings and willing to take responsibility for their actions. All these things are all highly visible to their contacts – which is why they're successful in building relationships and networks.

Body language or non-verbal methods of securing co-operation

Everyone knows that the way you dress can influence people. However, you can wear an expensive business suit and still not communicate confidence, empathy and, for networkers perhaps most importantly, sincerity. It's here that our body language and the visual signals we convey by our posture, eye contact, gestures and facial expression are crucial. Networkers must learn to control their body language if they wish to be successful. Visual signals can make you appear not to be in control, and will detract from your overall impression. Body language can often tell other people things about which you are not even aware.

Body language accounts for about 70% of what we communicate, with tone of voice and the actual words we use making up the other 30%. From the first moment you meet one of your contacts, they start to make judgements based on your body language. Their impression is based on what they see and not on what you say.

As with your self-esteem, body language is influenced by self-perception. Just as you can improve your self-esteem by changing your self-perception, you can also correct any negative body language by understanding your transferable skills, personal strengths, values and achievements. Accepting yourself for what you are, you'll be able to walk into any room full of confidence.

Some careers books advise you to stride into a room and take charge, asserting your personality to dazzle and impress. You're also encouraged to greet your contacts with vice-like handshakes and a hypnotic stare. Following this advice will guarantee that your contacts won't agree to a second meeting. Instead, be consistently yourself. First, prepare well for your meeting. This should make you feel confident, a fact that your contact will sense, and will help to get things off to a good start. As you enter the room, look directly at your contact and smile. This demonstrates that you're at ease. Smiling and eye contact are important, but should never appear forced. To make others feel comfortable you have to appear comfortable yourself.

Here are ten steps to better body language:

1. **Posture.** Sloppy posture conveys a lack of confidence and, possibly, a lack of discipline. When you meet your contact stand erect with your shoulders back. This will convey an alert and enthusiastic manner.

2. **Eye contact.** Eyes are very important in body language and are crucial in establishing rapport. Make eye contact before you speak and when your contact is speaking. Look away occasionally to avoid staring.

3. **Handshakes.** Shake hands firmly but don't hold the contact for too long.

4. **Seating.** Make sure you're comfortably seated. Keep your back straight and relax your breathing.

5. **Comfort zone.** People have a comfort zone that dictates how close they want other people to come, particularly when seated. Never invade your contact's space unless invited.

6. **Hands and arms.** Most problems with hands are caused by nervousness. Don't keep your hands in your pocket or fidget with rings, watches or cufflinks. Keep your hands away from your face. Don't put your hands behind your head – it's a

gesture used by the know-it-all. Avoid crossing your arms, this suggests that you have a closed attitude towards your contact.

7. **Leg gestures.** Crossed legs, like crossed arms, are often seen as a negative or defensive posture. Adopt a comfortable seating position, keeping your legs together and placing both feet on the ground without locking your ankles.

8. **Nodding agreement.** Using nods to punctuate key remarks made by your contact will signal agreement, interest and understanding.

9. **Smiling.** This is a positive signal to your contact and projects warmth. Most people look better when they smile, and it will make your contacts more comfortable because you'll appear natural and confident.

10. **Dress to suit the occasion.** Always maintain a good appearance and adapt your style of clothing to the occasion. If you're meeting a contact during the working day, then smart and formal would be appropriate. However, if the meeting is part of a social occasion, then informal and comfortable would be better.

MYTH BUSTER

Body language is only important when you're attending a job interview

Wrong! Understanding body language is important in every situation where you're communicating with other people. Your body is constantly sending out messages to other people to make very powerful statements about you, how you're feeling and what you're thinking. It's often the basis on which people decide whether or not you're worth listening to. Think of the many key roles for which an understanding of body language is important: these include selling, negotiating, counselling and networking.

JUDGEMENT

Networkers need to know how to exercise good judgement, a vital requirement when it comes to choosing your contacts, deciding who to keep and who to reject and with whom you should spend your valuable time. Judgement is partly intuitive and relates to our particular experience. At your first meeting with people, you'll often have to make quick-fire judgements about how much time to spend with them and whether it's worth arranging a follow-up meeting. You'll need to weigh up their credibility and whether they're likely to be of help to you in developing your career and job search.

OVERCOMING SHYNESS

To be successful in networking you need to overcome any natural shyness. To avoid feeling anxious or nervous when phoning or meeting your contacts, preparation is a must. Doing your homework before the meeting ensures that your thoughts are in order and boosts your confidence. As you've already discovered, the way you listen sends out messages about you, too. Listen with interest, focusing your eyes on the speaker. Animate your face with approval. It says, 'I'm with you and I'm interested in what you're saying'.

Once you've prepared for your meeting, you're well on the way to overcoming nervousness. You now need to concentrate on gaining physical and mental control of your nervousness: adjusting your attitude so that you have confidence and control of yourself.

You can also adjust your attitude to nervousness. What you say to yourself sends a message your listener receives. So select the attitude you want to communicate. Attitude adjusting is your mental suit of armour against nervousness. If you entertain only positive thoughts, you'll send out messages of naturalness, enthusiasm, sincerity, concern and authority.

Your initial meeting with a principal contact is always the hardest. However, following the advice set out here will ensure that things soon get easier.

PERSONAL MOTIVATION

Personal motivation is a skill. You need to be highly motivated to make a success of networking. This is not something you can take down from the shelf; you must *want* to network, because you can see just how important this is to your future and your career.

REMEMBER

✔ Communication is the key to successful networking, and the best networkers are outstanding communicators.

✔ To develop open supportive relationships you need to have the qualities of empathy, unqualified respect, integrity and acceptance.

✔ A lack of self-esteem or belief in yourself can hinder your ability to communicate effectively.

✔ You can improve your self-esteem by changing your self-perception. By focusing on your transferable skills, personal strengths, values and achievements, you can accentuate the positive and eliminate the negative.

✔ Always prepare what you want to say before meeting your contacts.

✔ For your networks to work effectively, you need the co-operation of your contacts.

✔ The verbal method of gaining co-operation, known as the 'assertive approach', is more likely to be successful in building relationships and networks.

✔ An effective networker must know how to master and control their body language if they wish to be successful.

✔ Networkers need to exercise good judgement in choosing their contacts.

✔ You need to be highly motivated to make a success of networking.

Networking for career change and job search

Using networking as a job-search technique can be highly effective. We know that around 80% of all vacancies are found in the hidden job market. Accessing this market using networking should therefore be a vital part of your career change or job-search strategy.

THE INFORMATIONAL MEETING

If you're reading this book because you need help with your job search, you may have already considered enlisting the help of other people. Begin by looking through your list of contacts to identify those who could be of most help. It's very important to include principal contacts who have strong networks of their own so that you have access to as many referred contacts as possible. Remember that the role of your principal contacts is to provide a doorway to company decision-makers, sources of information and spheres of influence.

Family, friends and social contacts

Divide your contacts into different groups (e.g. family and friends, social contacts, professional and business contacts), because you'll need to adopt a different approach for meeting contacts in each network. Contact people from your family and friends and social contacts networks by phone to arrange a meeting, but try not to explain your reasons at this point. Arrange to meet on neutral ground, such as a local pub or wine bar, where both you and your contact will feel relaxed.

At the meeting, after exchanging a few pleasantries, it's best to get straight down to business, since, if you keep up the friendly banter your contact may start to feel anxious. Explain that you need some help and guidance in finding your next job and ask if they could give you the names of anyone they know who'd be a suitable contact to approach. Stress that you're *not* going to ask them directly for a job, but rather for information that may lead to jobs and the names of other people who could help.

If your contacts don't already have a good idea of your experience and the type of job you're looking for, give them a brief outline. Don't pressure them to come up with names at the initial meeting; they may need time to consider your request. Instead, suggest that you'll give them a call in a few days' time, when you should establish as much information about these next contacts as possible, including the address and telephone number of their company and their job title. Finally, always send your friends and social contacts a short handwritten note after this meeting to thank them for their help.

Business and professional contacts

Just as with your other networks, begin by looking through your list of contacts, and choose those with wide-ranging networks of contacts of their own, who have a knowledge of your job and the industry in which you work. Make sure they can also offer you constructive advice and guidance.

A well-written letter is probably the best way to arrange a meeting, provided it's worded in such a way that your contact doesn't feel cornered or possibly under threat. Don't be tempted to use the direct approach and ask for a job. This is one way of guaranteeing that your supply of contacts dries up very quickly. Most people would feel very embarrassed at the prospect of being asked for a job without any preamble. Their predictable response would be a polite 'Sorry, but I'm too busy in the next few months to set up a meeting'. For the few who do manage to get a meeting using this approach, they can be sure their contact will not provide them with further names to add to the network, since they value their own reputation too greatly.

Networking can and does lead to job offers, but unless you understand its dynamics, you'll not succeed. If your principal contacts know they're only being approached for advice and guidance, they won't feel under threat and the meeting will be relaxed, with one person, the host, comfortably in the role of authority. Ultimately, the aim of networking for job-search purposes is not just to provide you with an endless list of contacts. At some point during your meetings with referred contacts, at first, second or third level, someone will be aware of a job that's right for you. By then they'll already be sufficiently interested in your background and experience to offer you the job.

Letters to your principal contacts should be well written and presented. Here are some general tips:

- Use good quality white A4 size paper of at least 100 gram.
- Draft and redraft your letter until you're satisfied with the content, keeping it to one side of an A4 sheet.
- Make sure your letters don't contain any mistakes and that the layout is always neat.
- It's essential to type these letters, preferably using a PC and word-processing software.
- Use first-class postage stamps.

Your letter should include an opening statement that will put your contact at ease. Explain your circumstances and go on to ask for help and guidance with your career. Follow this with a request for a short meeting. Here are several examples:

Tel: 020 7131 5432

27 Bellview Close
New Hampstead
London NW1 7PP

28 August 2000

Mr Peter Waitman
Marketing Manager
Lloyds Confectionery Company Ltd
Walpole Circular Road
London SE7 9VV

Dear Peter

When we last met, you were looking for some computer software to handle distribution problems. I hope that you've now found something suitable; if not, you may find the literature I'm enclosing helpful.

You may have read in the financial press that the annual profits of my employer, Jubilee Food Colourings, have fallen to an all-time low, and naturally I'm concerned that this may have an impact on jobs. I need to take advantage of your considerable knowledge of the industry and wondered if you could spare me 20 minutes for a meeting. I'm sure this will be of help in putting together my job-search strategy.

I know you're busy at the moment and I promise not to exceed the time limit. Could you take a look in your diary to find a convenient time and date? I'll give you a call in a few days to firm up the arrangement.

My best wishes to you and your family.

Mike Jordan

Mike Jordan

Tel: 01865 002312

16 Longford Terrace
North Bewley
Oxford OX9 2MM

25 October 2000

Mr Lawrence Jacobs
Facilities Manager
Oxford Security Instruments plc
Green Avenue
Oxford OX8 9LL

Dear Lawrence

I spoke to your secretary today and she tells me that you only returned to the office on Monday after a holiday with your wife in Thailand. I'm sure you've had a wonderful holiday, particularly when you appreciate how bad the weather has been in the UK.

Since we last met I've come to a crossroads in my career, and have decided the time is right to move to another company. I really need some advice and guidance on how I should go about the business of job search and would appreciate your help.

Could you spare me 20 minutes for a meeting at your offices? I'd be happy to make this during early November if this suits you. I'll give you a call in the next few days to firm up the arrangement.

My best wishes to you and your wife.

Pam Armstrong

Pam Armstrong

Tel: 01244 010188

34 Butterstone Road
Acres Wood
Chester CH7 2AZ

25 August 2000

Mr Richard Grey
Chief Engineer
Carloway Motor Parts
24 Eastchurch Road
Chester CH1 7YY

Dear Richard

I received the annual programme of events for the institute today, and the first thing I noticed was your appointment to the
chair of the Chester branch. Congratulations Richard, I'm confident that you'll make an excellent chairperson.

Strangely enough I too am looking for a boost to my career and
wondered if you might give me some advice. I have enclosed a
copy of my CV and would appreciate your comment on this and
whether it would benefit from some further improvement.

Could you spare me 20 minutes for a meeting at your offices?
I'd be happy to fit this in at the end of the day if this would help.
I'll give you a call soon to firm up the arrangement.

Kind regards

David Kerr

David Kerr

A meeting with your principal contact affords an ideal
opportunity to perfect the presentation of your career,
achievements and personal strengths. You'll also be able to
practise questions of your own.

Always begin these meetings by establishing rapport and
thanking your contact for agreeing to see you. A good
icebreaker is a topic that reflects your contact's interests,
or you could ask about business or family. Make sure this
isn't just a one-way discussion and don't dwell on this part

of your meeting for too long; simply use it as a bridge towards your objective. Remind your contact that you asked for this meeting because you need some help and guidance with your career. Reassure them that you're not there to ask for a job; this should take the pressure off the meeting and make your contact relax.

If you forwarded a copy of your CV before the meeting, ask for comment or recommendations for improvement. Always accept this advice even if you feel it may not help your cause, and answer any questions your contact may ask. If you didn't send your CV, then give your contact a brief account of your experience, including your major achievements. Throughout the meeting encourage questions and suggestions.

Explain to your contact that you need their help in obtaining the names of other contacts who would appreciate your experience, skills and achievements, even if they're not aware of suitable jobs. Reassure your contact that you won't ask their contacts for jobs. Otherwise, your contact is unlikely to co-operate.

Case Study
Networking success

Barbara, a 29 year-old legal executive, lost her job three weeks before Christmas after her employer announced that, because of a poor trading year, several people would be made redundant. This was Barbara's first job after qualifying and she had only worked for this company for two years.

Barbara was concerned about finding a new job. Not many vacancies were advertised and she had thought of networking but had dropped the idea because she had so few business contacts. Because Barbara was a keen swimmer and had been a member of her local swimming club for a long time, her boyfriend suggested she should talk to other club members about her situation. Reluctant, but also a little desperate by now, Barbara spoke to several club members and the club secretary.

Two weeks later Barbara received a call from the club secretary who put her in touch with an insurance manager, a colleague of his. After a meeting with this contact, and an interview with the company's area manager, Barbara was at last offered a job.

When your contact provides you with a list of other contacts, as a matter of courtesy, ask for permission to use their name for purposes of introduction. Aim to persuade your contact either to write to or phone their other contacts, since this is a very effective form of introduction. Even if the outcome isn't this productive, do make sure that you have their names, addresses and phone numbers, plus any other useful facts about these new contacts. Take a notebook with you and keep an account of all this information.

Before the meeting ends, ask your contact if you can offer any help in return, and whether you might keep them informed about your progress with the new contacts.

As soon as you get home, update your network directory with the information you've obtained and send a short thank-you letter. Here's an example:

Tel: 020 7131 5432

27 Bellview Close
New Hampstead
London NW1 7PP

15 September 2000

Mr Peter Waitman
Marketing Manager
Lloyds Confectionery Company Ltd
Walpole Circular Road
London SE7 9VV

Dear Peter

Thank you for agreeing to see me on Tuesday last. I appreciate very much the advice you gave me to further my career, and the names of colleagues who may also be able to help.

I'll be writing to these people in the next few days and will make a point of keeping you aware of developments.

Kindest regards

Mike Jordan

Mike Jordan

THE IMPORTANCE OF RESEARCH

Before you set about arranging meetings with referred contacts, you should find out as much information about the company as possible.

To help with your research, larger public libraries, universities and business school libraries often house extensive collections of reference material. However, it's always worth checking out your local library first. Make sure that your research is well organised and that you have your network directory to hand for recording any information. Keep a note of the sources of information you've studied, filing any newspaper cuttings, articles and photocopies.

Here's a list of publications that can be found in larger public libraries:

- *The Times 1000.* This is a directory of the top 1,000 largest UK companies, ranked by turnover. Contains data on size, main activity, number of employees and key personnel. Published by Times Books.
- *The Personnel Manager's Yearbook.* Lists prominent companies, with names of personnel and human resource executives and a useful directory of recruitment specialists. Published by A. P. Information Services.
- *Who Owns Whom.* A cross-referencing of interlocking holdings and affiliations. Volume one indexes parent companies followed by subsidiaries. Volume two lists subsidiaries followed by their parent company. Updated quarterly. Published by Dun and Bradstreet.
- *Confederation of Chambers of Commerce Directory.* Each directory covers the specific part of the country in which you live and lists names of member companies of all sizes, together with their contact name, address, telephone number and activity. Some libraries have these in their reference section.

- *Kelly's Business Directory.* Contains information on over 82,000 industrial, commercial and professional organisations in the UK. Provides name, address, telephone number and a brief description. Published by Kelly's Directories.
- *Whitaker's Almanac.* Useful if you need information on employers, societies and institutions, trade associations and unions, industrial research centres, the press, banks, etc. Published by J. Whitaker and Sons Ltd.
- *Handbook of Market Leaders.* Who's on top, sector by sector. Published by Extel Financial Ltd.

There'll almost certainly be a trade magazine covering the industry in which you are interested. Ask your library if they have any copies. Professional magazines published for members of a particular profession are also a useful source of company information. If you're not already receiving a professional magazine, again ask your public library if they have a copy.

You may also find copies of annual reports for larger companies in your public library. However, these will only be for companies in your particular region. Alternatively, phone the company you're interested in and ask their public relations department to send you a copy.

Most companies produce sales leaflets detailing the products or services they offer. These can provide you with some very useful background information to the company. Ask the public relations department to send you a selection with the copy of the annual report.

The Internet is rapidly becoming an important source of information. Even small companies have a website, where a lot of the information you're seeking can be found. Profiles of the company usually contain information such as details of its products or services, names of senior management and useful addresses and telephone numbers. Larger companies will provide a link to a designated recruitment page with details of current vacancies.

A list of useful search engines with their website addresses can be found in the resource directory at the back of this book. If you don't have the website address for the company you're researching, try a 'keyword' search on one of these search engines.

National newspapers including *The Times, Daily Telegraph* and *Observer* all have websites where you can obtain recent company information using a keyword search. These newspapers provide comprehensive information on CD-ROM for a quarterly subscription. Again, it's worth asking at larger public libraries whether they can provide this service.

Using these sources of information, try to build up a picture of the company that includes the following information:

- Full name and address, telephone, fax number and e-mail address of the company's head office. Locations of other company premises.
- The name of any holding company or group.
- The names and titles of directors or senior managers, including the senior human resources post.
- What the company makes, or the services it provides.
- Whether the company is family owned, private or publicly held.
- How long the company has been established.
- Sales turnover and staff numbers.
- Recent company developments, acquisitions or mergers.

MEETINGS WITH REFERRED CONTACTS

In terms of preparation, this meeting is no less important than a job interview. Pay the same level of attention to your personal presentation and appearance. The referred contact may well have a suitable vacancy and will certainly be assessing whether you're a suitable person to pass on to other business colleagues. Making a strong impact at this stage may also benefit you later, since your contacts are far more likely to remember you when they hear about a suitable vacancy. How you conduct yourself in front of this contact can mean the difference between a job offer and just another meeting.

To arrange meetings with referred contacts you need to write to them first. It's important to begin such letters with a reference to your principal contact who recommended the approach. Next, explain your need for career advice and then ask for a short meeting. Enclose a copy of your CV and refer to it briefly to reinforce the important aspects of your career so far, your experience and achievements. Conclude the letter by stating that you'll contact them in a few days to arrange the meeting. Here is an example:

Tel: 020 7131 5432   27 Bellview Close
                                                New Hampstead
                                                London NW1 7PP

17 September 2000

Mr P D Wells
Finance Director
Medway Communications Ltd
122–126 Redhill Road
London SW7 8QQ

Dear Mr Wells

My name is Mike Jordan, and I'm writing to you today at the suggestion of Peter Waitman of Lloyds Confectionery to ask if you could spare me a little of your time for a meeting to help with my career.

You may be aware from the financial press that my employer Jubilee Food Colourings haven't had a good trading year, and naturally I'm concerned that this may have an impact on jobs. I would very much like your advice on possible career moves and the names of others you may recommend I should contact for help. Enclosed is a copy of my CV, which you may care to look at before our meeting. To summarise my background, I am a qualified accountant with some eight years' experience, the last three of these in a senior position with Jubilee Food Colourings.

I appreciate that you have many commitments and thank you in anticipation of spending 20 minutes to cover the points mentioned above. I'll give you a call in the next few days to firm up the arrangement for our meeting.

Yours sincerely

Mike Jordan

Mike Jordan

Your referred contact may be used to getting quite a lot of letters requesting an interview. Normally, they would never read such letters, because a secretary would have redirected them to the company's human resource department. However, because you made sure the personal recommendation appeared in the first sentence of your letter, the secretary will pass the letter to her boss for action. Your contact will feel compelled to see you for fear of offending the friend and business contact who recommended you.

Set the agenda

Once the meeting has been arranged, go through your research material again to refresh your memory. Prepare beforehand what you want to discuss with your contact. Here's a suggested agenda:

- *Summarise your background and experience.* If you've included a personal profile in your CV, it's a good idea to use this, expanding on your key selling points.
- *Discuss your new skills and relevant experience.* Describe some of your recent accomplishments and highlight the transferable skills and personal strengths which you believe your contact would find most interesting. Use examples. Make clear your career goals and objectives.
- *Foster dialogue.* Ask questions and draw information from your contact.
- *Ask questions.* Prepare questions in advance. The more specific, the better.
- *Get referrals.*
- *Be sensitive to your contact's needs.*

'The most common mistake people make when networking is not preparing adequately for networking meetings. Deciding what you want to discuss with your contacts is essential.'
Managing human resources consultant

Meeting your contact

When you first meet your contact, make eye contact, smile and look confident. Thank them for agreeing to the meeting and reiterate that you'd appreciate some help and guidance with your career. Your contact may well be suspicious about the real reason for the meeting, but don't let this affect your relationship. Take the initiative and explain that a good starting point would be to spend a few minutes summarising your background and experience, together with your most recently acquired skills and accomplishments, set against your career objectives. This part of your presentation is best prepared and practised well in advance of the meeting.

When you've finished, invite your contact to ask questions. Get feedback on your career goals, job-search plan and CV. If they mention any obstacles you might face in reaching your career goal, ask for advice on how to overcome them. If your contact cannot help, ask for the name of someone who might be able to give you the information you need.

Try to find an opportunity to let your contact know that you've done some homework on their company. For example, say 'I see you're branching out into new products' or 'I recently read that you are opening new offices'. 'Could you tell me a little more about it?' Most people will be happy to discuss their company, and you'll be getting a lot of valuable information, including how this might affect your career opportunities.

Be sure to ask your prepared questions and listen to the answers to ensure two-way communication. Acknowledge and respond to what your contact is saying. By following your contact's cues, you can determine what interests them the most. If they show signs of uneasiness, quickly change the subject.

During this discussion, you may discover that the company does indeed need someone with your skills and experience. If so, ask your contact if you could meet with someone closer to the action. If you've created sufficient interest, your contact will consider this a good idea. If not, this can only mean that they have someone else in mind for the job or your introduction has not struck the right note. If this is the case, don't force yourself on the contact any further.

When your contact has finished talking about the company, thank them for the information and explain that you're looking for some other like-minded employers where your skills and experience would be a good fit. Ask your contact for the names of other contacts and their companies or search and recruitment consultants so that you can approach them in a similar way. Be sure to get sufficient information about these referred contacts before leaving the meeting.

Networking meetings are about mutuality, so ask your contact if there's anything you can do to help them. Being sensitive in this way tends to imprint the meeting in the contact's mind.

At this point, you've achieved your objective. You've presented yourself to your contact as a potential employee for his company and have elicited the names of further contacts. Don't be disappointed that you haven't been offered a job. It can happen, but it's most unlikely so early on in your networking. Your chances of meeting someone with a suitable vacancy will improve as you move deeper into the network.

At the conclusion of your meeting, thank your contact for their help and guidance, and reassure them that you'll get on well with the people they have referred you to. Promise to keep your contact informed about your future career moves. Remember that this process of nurturing your contacts will sustain and enhance your career.

> 'Some people only go through the motions of networking and making contacts. It's not enough to just meet someone for 20 minutes. What you say and how you present yourself can make a big difference to whether you're successful or not at networking.'
>
> *Career management specialist*

When you return home, update your network directory with the information gathered from the meeting, prepare a letter of thanks for your referred contact (see the earlier example) and send a letter to your principal contact to bring them up to date. Here's an example:

Tel: 020 7131 5432

28 September 2000

27 Bellview Close
New Hampstead
London NW1 7PP

Mr Peter Waitman
Marketing Manager
Lloyds Confectionery Company Ltd
Walpole Circular Road
London SE7 9VV

Dear Peter

Just to let you know that I've had a most useful meeting with Philip Wells of Medway Communications. He gave me some very good ideas and names of useful contacts. I'll be arranging to see these people shortly.

I really do appreciate your help in getting this far with my career development and I'm most grateful.

Kind regards

Mike Jordan

Mike Jordan

You now have a further layer of referred contacts who should be treated in exactly the same way as the first layer. Prepare suitable letters and away you go!

MYTH BUSTER

Networking meetings are nothing more than an opportunity to flatter the other person

Wrong! If this were the purpose of networking meetings, then valuable contacts would be lost very quickly. Most people see through flattery for what it is — insincerity. Flattery must not be confused with empathy, which is taking a genuine interest in your contacts and seeing the world from their point of view. Also, never forget that your contacts have entered into a relationship based on trust and mutuality.

YOUR CV

Should you send a copy of your CV (curriculum vitae) when writing to referred contacts? This very much depends on whether your contact could be of direct help with your job search. Some may see the inclusion of a CV as worrying proof that you're going to ask them for a job. Ask your principal contact whether this would be a good idea or not.

In most cases, if the referred contacts have good networks of their own, they'll find a CV helpful and will appreciate the fact that having this information in advance should reduce the length of your meeting.

Case Study
You're never too old to network!

Peter, a 55 year-old accountant, found himself out of work when his company was taken over by a large American corporation. His first move, typical of many professional people, was to contact several recruitment consultants in London. His CV was politely acknowledged but nothing further happened for five weeks. Peter then telephoned the recruitment consultants and they all said that his age made him a difficult candidate to place.

After telling one of his friends what had happened, Peter decided to change his strategy and began to network with personal and business contacts. He was surprised at just how many people he knew. One of these, a long-term supplier to his previous employer, put him in touch with three referred contacts. Some six weeks later he came face to face with the managing director of a small printing company and was offered a job.

Whilst his starting salary was less than with his previous employer, Peter realised this wasn't so important. He'd been given a generous redundancy package and his monetary needs were far less because his children had flown the nest.

CONTACTS IN THE RECRUITMENT BUSINESS

It's a good idea to build contacts with those people in the recruitment business who can help you with your career change or job search. Employers may use one of the following to help them recruit staff:

- headhunters, sometimes known as search consultants (usually targeting the top 5% of the job market)
- recruitment consultants
- employment and recruitment agencies.

Headhunters

If you're contacted by a headhunter, it means that their research has identified you as a person who possesses the special skills, qualifications and experience to fill a particular job for one of their clients. The headhunter will ask whether you can talk: after all, you may be in a room filled with people. If you can, they'll tell you that you're being considered for a senior post. You'll be given brief information about the post, its level and reporting relationship, why the appointment is being made and the industry in which their client is based. You won't be given the name of the client or any information on salary and benefits, since this remains confidential for the time being. You may be asked a few questions to confirm the information the headhunter has obtained about your experience and qualifications, although a good deal may already be known about you. At this point, if the headhunter is satisfied they will ask you to attend an interview.

Although headhunters keep files on potential candidates, these are usually the people *they* have identified, and not candidates who have sent their CV on a speculative basis. However, you must get your CV on the headhunters' files. This isn't an easy task, because their daily post-bags bulge with similar CVs, not all of which are even kept in their files. By far the best way to make contact with the headhunter is through networking. To do this you need to locate a human resource manager or managing director as your principal or referred contact. At your first meeting with the contact ask for the names of other contacts, in particular any headhunters who could help. If your contact has handled recruitment and selection at a senior level, then they'll probably be able to give you a suitable name. Ask your contact if they'd be prepared to contact the headhunter on your behalf. This prepares the consultant for your call and eases the introduction considerably. Try to find out when your contact intends to make the call, since you don't want to get in touch with the consultant before your contact has had a chance to do their part.

To fix the arrangement in the mind of the headhunter, send them a letter first stating that you're writing at the request of your contact. You should be granted a meeting, since it's highly unlikely that they would refuse a request from someone who was being introduced by one of their major clients. Allow a few days to pass, then give the headhunter a call to arrange the meeting.

Here's a sample of this type of letter:

Tel: 020 7891 8889   17 Sycamore Terrace
                                            Wimbledon
                                            London SW19 7RT

30 September 2000

Mr Brian Welton
Managing Consultant
Gordon White Search Co. Ltd
Bell Street
London SW1 9EE

Dear Mr Welton

My name is Roy Davison, and I'm writing to you today at the suggestion of Mr John Butler, the human resource manager of FRP
Finance company, to ask if you could spare me a little of your
time for a meeting to help with my career.

I have extensive experience in Public Relations and have included
a copy of my CV for your information. At this point in my career,
I believe the time is right to move into a more demanding and
satisfying role with a better salary and benefits package.

I'll call you soon to make a convenient arrangement.

Kind regards

Roy Davison

Roy Davison

Recruitment consultants

Unlike headhunters, recruitment consultants advertise
vacancies on behalf of their clients. Whilst headhunters
may introduce a good candidate to one of their clients on
a speculative basis, recruitment consultants are only
concerned with filling vacancies notified to them by their
clients. Whilst some recruitment consultants offer a
comprehensive service, handling all responses, carrying out
initial interviews, administering selection tests and drawing
up a shortlist, others may just sift out candidates based
largely on the evidence of CVs or short interviews.
Networking with recruitment consultants is no

different than with headhunters. However, they're certainly easier to contact direct if it's not possible to be referred by one of their clients.

You should target those recruitment consultants who maintain a database of candidates. Ask your local library if they have a copy of *The CEPEC Recruitment Guide* or *The Executive Grapevine*. Both these publications contain lists of headhunters and recruitment consultants, with details of their particular specialisation and whether speculative applications are accepted. Contact names to whom your CV can be addressed are also provided. You'll need to send a covering letter with your CV. Here's an example:

Tel: 020 7678 4356

116 Garner Street
Chiswick
London W2L 7BB

26 March 2000

Mr Alan Beamer
Choice & Partners (Search Consultants)
24–26 New Cross Road
London W3L 6GG

Dear Mr Beamer

I have twelve years' experience in the field of facilities management and was appointed to the post of Facilities Manager with a large hospital group in 1992. I have decided to seek new opportunities, and have included a copy of my CV on the chance that you may be working on an assignment that could use a professionally qualified Facilities Manager. My strongest skills include negotiating contracts, site management and health and safety.

I would welcome the opportunity of a short meeting, say twenty minutes, to bring you up to scratch on my skills and personal strengths. I will give your office a call in a week's time to arrange this.

Yours sincerely

Tony Adamson

Tony Adamson

Employment and recruitment agencies

Employment agencies are keen to encourage applicants to register their career details so that they can be contacted when a suitable vacancy arises. They handle a large spread of jobs from entry level up to middle management. Look in your local *Yellow Pages* or *Thomson Directory* for details of employment agencies, and telephone them first to make sure they recruit the job you're looking for. Ideally, give the agency a copy of your CV as part of an exploratory interview, and only as a last resort send them a copy by post. A meeting with a member of the agency staff is important, because you can use the opportunity to market yourself. Find some common ground with whoever interviews you and establish a rapport with them. In this way, they're more likely to work at placing you with one of their clients. Keep the networking channel open and telephone your contact at your chosen employment agencies about every three weeks just to see if there have been any new vacancies.

NETWORKING FOR THE UNEMPLOYED

If you're unemployed or about to lose your job, you may well feel the need to inject a real sense of urgency into your job-search plans. Maximise your chances of securing your next job by using every source available to you and in particular exploit the hidden job market by networking. You may be thinking that it's too late to start networking, particularly if you've been unemployed for several months. However, it's never too late to begin. Keep in mind that the hidden job market accounts for 80% of the available vacancies and networking is the most productive source of vacancies in this market.

Because you're unemployed, your job search will be a full-time job in itself, so why not begin the process now by identifying and listing your principal contacts? The sooner you get some networking meetings arranged, the sooner you'll feel that something is really happening.

There's no reason why you shouldn't apply for

advertised vacancies whilst you're networking, so long as you understand the value of identifying your transferable skills, personal strengths and achievements and put in the most effort where the most vacancies can be found. The resource directory at the end of this book contains a list of national newspapers that carry job vacancies.

REMEMBER

✔ Identify principal contacts who have strong networks of their own so that you have access to as many referred contacts as possible.

✔ Arrange meetings with family and friends and social contacts on neutral ground where both of you will feel relaxed.

✔ Send your friends and social contacts a short handwritten note after this meeting to thank them for their help.

✔ A well-written letter is the best method of arranging a meeting with your professional and business contacts.

✔ This is the ideal opportunity to perfect the presentation of your career, achievements and personal strengths.

✔ Immediately you return home, update your network directory.

✔ Before you arrange a meeting with referred contacts, carry out some research.

✔ Spend a few minutes talking about yourself and your background. Invite your contact to ask questions. Let them know that you've done some homework on their company.

✔ When you return home, update your network directory. Send a letter of thanks to your referred contact and one to your principal contact to bring them up to date.

Targeting specific employers

IDENTIFYING SUITABLE EMPLOYERS

Another approach to networking is to target specific employers on a speculative basis. To begin with, your targeting will involve identifying and researching those organisations that are most likely to employ people with your skills and experience. Secondly, you will need to identify a key person within the organisation to whom you can direct your approach.

If you are unsure of specific organisations to approach, you must carry out some general research looking at the industry in which you are interested.

Current directories with information about particular industries to be found in public libraries include:

- *British Rate and Data (BRAD)*. A directory of business publications.
- *Kompass UK (Register of British Industry & Commerce)*. In seven volumes, this is an exhaustive guide to 40,000 British companies, identifying them by geographical location, products and services and describing in tabular form what sort of trading activities they undertake. Published by Reed Information Services Ltd.
- *Macmillan Directory of Business Information Sources*. Gives details of the leading 10,000 unquoted companies registered in Great Britain, including subsidiaries of well-known companies, which are not quoted on the Stock Exchange.
- *Key British Enterprises*. Lists the top 20,000 British companies, showing the address, type of activity, when founded, names of directors and sales turnover. Published by Dun and Bradstreet.

- *Directory of Trade Associations and Professional Bodies in the UK*. Provides details of names, addresses, telephone numbers and descriptions of trade associations and professional bodies. Published by Gale Research International.
- *Directory of British Associations*. Published by CBD Research Ltd.

CRITERIA FOR FINAL SELECTION

From these directories, compile a list of the companies in the industry in which you are interested. Using the sources described in Chapter 4 under the section 'The importance of research', your research should now become much more focused. Rank the companies of your choice in their order of importance to you, and choose the top five or six to research in detail. Use the following criteria to select these companies:

- Which of these companies is a good match for your personal values? Are you looking for a small or large company? A relatively new or well-established company? Manufacturer or service provider? Do the companies have pay and benefits that are a good match for your needs? Are these companies in the geographical area of your choice?
- Do these companies have strict rules of recruitment and selection, or are they relaxed in their approach? If they have strict rules applying to age, skills and qualifications etc., do you satisfy all these requirements?
- Do these companies recruit using selection tests, assessment centres? Do they use recruitment consultants, their own human resource department or is recruitment in the hands of individual line managers?

This criteria helps to determine whether your chosen companies have barriers that can make a speculative approach difficult. Ideally, you should focus on companies that show evidence of filling vacancies outside of the standard methods.

Armed with your research, you can prepare a suitably worded letter to a named individual at the company of your choice. Make sure that the person you've identified as your contact is still with the company and still in the same position. Call the company and ask the switchboard. If your contact is no longer with the company, explain that you need to update your records and could they give you the name of the person now occupying that position. Make sure you spell the contact's name correctly.

The purpose of this letter is to let them know that you have a genuine interest in the company; you can do this by referring to some of the material from your research findings. Next, don't ask for a job; instead, use the standard networking approach and ask for a short meeting to help with your career. Enclose a copy of your CV, but stress that you'd value your contact's opinion on your suitability for a particular job. Here's an example of this type of letter:

Tel: 0161 444 1100   24 Bakers Lane
                                       Stamford
                                       Manchester M55 8TD

25 August 2000

Mr Paul Fox
Production Director
Maple Soft Drinks Co. Ltd
89–95 Claris Road
Manchester M88 9RR

Dear Mr Fox

Because of my interest in your company, I recently requested a copy of your 1999 annual report and discovered from this that you anticipate introducing a much greater level of technology into your production process during the next three years. This prompted me to research your company further and my findings confirmed that you've been particularly successful in both producing and selling your products.

As a computer programmer with several years' experience of working with other technical staff on production development issues, I'd very much appreciate your help and guidance with my career. Could you spare me 20 minutes of your time for a meeting? I've enclosed a copy of my CV, which you may care to glance at before our meeting.

I'll give you a call in a few days' time to discuss arrangements for our meeting.

Yours sincerely

Christopher Jones

Christopher Jones

'I can never understand why some people go to all the trouble of asking for a meeting to help with their job search when they know almost nothing about the company. Why should I help someone who's not even prepared to spend some of their time looking for this information?'

Human resource manager – building industry

PHONING YOUR CONTACT

When you phone your contact, be prepared for your call to be intercepted by a secretary. Most secretaries are well trained to screen unwanted calls from their boss. Try calling around 8am and you just might get through directly. If your call is intercepted, you're bound to be asked about the nature of your call. Explain that you recently wrote to their boss asking for an appointment and that they're expecting your call. This should get you through to your contact. If it doesn't and you're told that their boss is busy and will return your call later, don't accept this suggestion, because they probably won't ring back. Instead, ask when would be a good time to phone again. Hopefully, the secretary will suggest a more convenient time.

Despite your charm and persuasiveness, however, there will be times when you won't get through. In such cases maintain a friendly relationship with the secretary and thank them for their help. Remember, they could be a useful ally. All you can do now is find someone else who can act as a bridge to your contact. You could try contacting a manager from the same company or ask at your local institute meetings whether anyone knows your contact.

If you do manage to speak to your contact, be polite but positive. Begin by saying that you're calling about your recent letter asking for some career advice. When would be a convenient time and day for the meeting? Be prepared to give your contact some more information should they request it.

> 'If you manage to get through to your contact on the telephone, but he's perhaps too busy to meet with you, ask if there's someone else in the organisation who would be free to help you. Meeting with this person may prove to be very useful and you can then think about using this person as a bridge to your original contact.'
>
> *Sales director – plant and machinery hire industry*

MEETINGS WITH TARGETED EMPLOYERS

The format for your meeting is identical to the one used in meetings with referred contacts (see previous chapter). Here's a summary of the format:

- Thank your contact for the meeting.
- Summarise your background and experience, together with recently acquired skills and accomplishments (practise this well in advance of the meeting).
- Invite your contact to ask questions and get feedback on your career goals.
- Ask for advice on how to overcome obstacles.
- Tell your contact what you know about their company (make sure that you have plenty of information from your research to back up the content of your letter).

- Ask your prepared questions.
- If the company has a suitable vacancy, ask for a further introduction.
- Ask for the names and details of other contacts.
- Ask your contact if there is anything you can do to help them in return.
- Finally, thank your contact once again for the meeting.

When you return home, update your network directory with the information gathered from the meeting and prepare a letter of thanks.

Case Study

One door closes, another opens

Allison worked as a shop manager, but lost her job when her employer decided to close her shop along with several others in the same area.

Married with a young child, Allison couldn't afford to wait very long before securing her next job. She decided to ask her employer if they knew of other employers in the same line of business. Allison's employer was very positive in responding to her request and, because of her excellent work record, was willing to introduce her to several people known to the area manager. Allison recalled that knowing something about her present employer had been the key to getting the job, so she met her area manager and asked for background information about each of his contacts.

All of Allison's networking meetings went well, but no one was able to offer her a job because there were no vacancies at the time. Four weeks after leaving her job as shop manager, Allison received a telephone call from one of the contacts she had previously met. He asked her to call in to see him later that day and offered her a job she was very keen to accept.

REMEMBER

✔ If you're unsure of specific organisations to approach, then carry out some general research about the industry in which you are interested.

✔ From your list of companies, choose the top five or six to research in detail.

✔ Use the criteria provided to help determine which of your chosen companies have barriers that could make a speculative approach difficult.

✔ In your letter let your contact know that you have a genuine interest in the company and use the standard networking approach of asking for a short meeting. Enclose a copy of your CV.

✔ When you speak to your contact on the telephone, be prepared to give more information before your request is agreed to.

✔ The format for this meeting is identical to that used in meetings with referred contacts (see previous chapter).

✔ Make sure that you have plenty of information from your research to back up the content of your letter.

✔ When you return home, update your network directory.

THE IMPORTANCE OF LEARNING

Whatever your current situation, whether you're a manager with many years' experience or a young person just starting out on your career path, there's one thing you must do to protect your career – take personal responsibility for your continuing education.

In this fast-changing world of ours, it doesn't take long for skills and knowledge to become outdated. Technology is progressing at an incredible rate and this makes it extremely difficult to keep up to date. Management theories and practices change, whilst craft and skilled workers must learn constantly to adapt to new techniques. Clearly, we can't let progress pass us by. We must learn to re-equip ourselves continually and become lifelong students; otherwise, we risk serious permanent damage to our careers.

Continuing education and learning is the only way to keep your career fresh and your job-search prospects at their best. Of course, your employer might help you with this, but ultimately, it's your responsibility to manage your self-development and your career. You could say your future employability depends upon it. Building relationships inside and outside your company and making the most of your networking skills can play an important part in your continuing education and personal development.

MYTH BUSTER

If employers want to keep their staff, they must provide all the training they need

Wrong! Whilst some employers are willing to provide training in certain aspects of their business, this isn't enough to guarantee future employability. Also, employers don't have the funds to provide comprehensive training and development for their staff.

You need to take responsibility for your own learning and development if you wish to protect your career. Attend courses, study exams, read books and generally keep abreast of what's happening in your field.

WHAT SHOULD YOU BE LEARNING?

What exactly then should you be learning to keep your career in good shape? This can be summed up as learning new skills and maintaining an awareness of new developments in your chosen field. New skills can include anything that makes you a more well-rounded person: for example, supervisory skills, familiarity with technology (including the Internet), accounting and finance skills, commercial awareness, communication skills, health and safety, and personal skills such as assertiveness. Keep abreast of changes and developments within your chosen profession. For example, if you're a human resource officer, then you must make sure you know about all the changes to employment law. If you're a craft or skilled person, such as an electrician, then you must study and take the examinations for the most recent electrical regulations. It really doesn't matter whether you teach, work with computers, nurse sick people or manage a garden centre, you need specialist knowledge and you must keep this up to date.

'Career development through learning is fast becoming the only insurance policy employees have to protect their careers and their future.'

Managing director – automotive industry

Whilst continuing education and personal development is undoubtedly an investment, it also means making a personal sacrifice. This may involve allocating your personal time for study or working without payment.

HOW NETWORKING CAN HELP YOUR DEVELOPMENT

Just as you can use self-marketing and developing networks to help with career change and job search, both can be employed proactively to generate help for your continuing education and development.

People are often wary about networking in this way, because they believe it may signal to their employer that they're planning to leave or that discussing their accomplishments and personal strengths at work may be seen as boasting. Put all of these concerns to one side, because networking can also benefit your employer. If you're regularly dealing with customers, your networking skills will produce orders and your relationship with suppliers will enable worthwhile discounts to be applied. As you build up your networks, your personal skills will also improve and you'll become a more effective employee.

You can work on your continuing education and career development by ensuring that the important people in your organisation know about your transferable skills, achievements and career objectives. One obvious way of achieving this is through performance appraisal. If your employer has an appraisal scheme and there is a regular review of your performance against targets, then your immediate boss and their boss should be aware of your achievements and career plans. Unfortunately, many appraisal schemes only occur once a year at a meeting with the employee's superior. From everyone's viewpoint, this is far from satisfactory.

MENTORS

Contacts within your own organisation also form part of your professional and business network. Using the skills discussed in Chapter 3, you can build up a useful network of contacts. From these, select one contact who has a strong professional reputation in your organisation as your mentor. Mentoring is a relatively recent management development technique where an employee with potential is put under the wing of a middle or senior manager to be given advice and to increase their experience and business ability. As well as acting as a guide to your work performance, a mentor will help you to focus more clearly on your career objectives. Your career objectives sometimes become realistic objectives, because your mentor can get you the right degree of exposure in the organisation and put you forward for promotion.

The advantages of having a mentor are obvious. The awareness and understanding that a professional and more experienced person can bring will contribute greatly to your continuing education and development. A mentor can also be extremely valuable in introducing you to contacts in their own personal network. Most people are flattered to take on the role of mentor, since it gives them recognition as an expert in their field.

If you're unable to find someone willing to become a mentor, you could ask one person or several people to spare some time to coach you on what is happening in your organisation and industry, the latest business theories and generally to give you feedback on work performance. Choose these people just as carefully as you would a mentor. However, because they're not fully committed to assuming this role, you must take the initiative to manage and control the timing and frequency of your coaching.

Most people will be prepared to spare some time to give you advice and guidance in a coaching role. However, never put them under pressure, and be prepared to assess the ability of the person you intend to ask. You may embarrass them if they're forced to admit that they can't help you.

Use their time wisely and know what you want before you ask. Always be specific; if you're vague, you may end up getting information you don't really need.

MYTH BUSTER

Mentors can only be appointed by your employer

Wrong! Whilst mentors can be appointed by your employer if you're on a fast-track promotion scheme, there's nothing to stop you finding someone willing to take on this role. Ideally, ask someone from within your own organisation, but if this fails, you can ask someone from outside, provided they work within the industry you've selected for your career.

BUILDING YOUR VISIBILITY

Meetings

Achieving visibility within your organisation is an important part of self-marketing and career development. Most people are quite content to spend all their working life in their chosen profession without ever finding out what people or other departments do. As an active networker, why not take the initiative and suggest to your manager that you could make a short presentation about your department and your role to other areas of the business? Not only will this help to improve your presentation skills but also you'll be raising your visibility, making others aware of your skills and creating the opportunity to add further contacts to your network.

If you're asked to attend internal meetings, try to get hold of a copy of the agenda in good time. Familiarise yourself with the minutes of the previous meeting and the people who'll be attending. Depending on the subject matter, you could volunteer either to chair the meeting or speak about one of the agenda items. Even if this isn't possible, research the agenda items and make sure that you participate as actively as possible in the meeting. To avoid getting a reputation as someone who merely challenges everything, do your homework before the meeting, speak with authority and make a positive contribution.

Maintaining an awareness of office politics is also important, since you don't want to get involved in an argument or upset the very person you're keen to impress by a careless remark. Always arrive early so that you can choose to sit where you can easily be seen and heard by the decision-makers. During the meeting always portray positive body language and look out for positive and negative signals from others. Refresh your understanding of body language by reading about the subject in Chapter 3.

Exhibitions and trade shows

Another very effective way of presenting yourself to people is through exhibitions and trade shows. Many companies use these to sell their products and services and to raise the public's general awareness. If your organisation intends to book space at one of these events, ask if you might be included on the stand, even if only to act as a relief for someone during lunch. There you'll meet a lot of people and find plenty of opportunities to exchange business cards.

Training courses

Many companies have dedicated training staff. However, opportunities sometimes arise to give presentations on courses such as induction training for new employees, or you could deliver training to staff on a new product or service you've developed. Alternatively, you may be asked to participate in training some of your customers. Show a willingness to get involved in training, even if this means you have to work that much harder to keep your own work up to date. Needless to say, you should take every opportunity to attend training courses and seminars yourself.

Public speaking

Of course, you needn't limit your visibility to within your own organisation; there are plenty of other opportunities for public speaking on behalf of your company. You could, for example, deliver a speech about your company to Rotary Clubs or make an after-dinner speech at a company social occasion.

All of this requires public-speaking skills that can't be learned overnight. However, you can make a point of watching other speakers and learning from them. Don't bite off more than you can chew at the beginning. Practise in front of a few people; in this way you can build up your skill and confidence. The requirements for public speaking include:

- confidence
- plenty of preparation
- understanding your audience
- getting your timing right
- enthusiasm
- creating audience participation
- preparing for questions
- learning voice control
- using positive body language
- learning to speak without a script
- when appropriate, some humour
- ending on a high note.

There are a number of books on the subject of public speaking and the titles of some of these can be found in the resource directory at the back of this book.

Charity and community work

A very useful way of raising your visibility is to undertake charity or community work on behalf of your company. Many employers now recognise that they should put something back into the local community. You could organise fund-raising events or volunteer some of your free time to help a local school or theatre. Why not think about becoming a school governor? Be prepared for some of these things to be newsworthy with the media taking an interest.

> 'It used to be considered enough to progress if you kept your head down and did a good job; recognition would come eventually. Today, this job style would lead to falling back in the career stakes. You need to take every opportunity to market yourself, making others aware of your skills and achievements.'
> *General manager, career development − insurance industry*

Writing articles for newsletters and magazines

Writing articles for your company magazine can bring you to the attention of others. Ask your public relations department if they would be interested in an article about some interesting aspect of your work.

If you're a member of a professional institute, they're sure to produce a newsletter at branch level. Send them an article about a new development in the industry or a letter commenting on some new legislation, etc.

LATERAL MOVES

Until the 1980s, promotion was always thought to be a vertical process − working steadily up the career ladder. Large organisations operating in this way were often described as pyramid organisations with vertical career paths. With their many layers of both management and staff, people progressed slowly but surely, and able performers could expect to be offered good long-term career prospects by their employer.

During the 1980s, organisations encountered difficulties brought about by the recession. Companies had little choice other than to reduce their costs and the size of their workforce. Many reacted by shedding staff, often taking out entire layers, particularly of management. As a result, there were fewer promotion opportunities.

Organisations began to move away from vertical career paths to a structure where employees were more likely to advance their career by moving laterally. There was also a strong feeling in the human resource profession that employees would make better senior managers if they had gained wide-ranging experience in several functions rather than just one.

Why would you want to make a lateral move? Perhaps your current position no longer fits in well with your career objectives, or maybe you recognise that some additional skills would be helpful in achieving your objectives. You may also believe that moving to a more high-profile department would put you in a better position for promotion, or that the future of your employer's business lies in a different department.

Increasing internal job mobility also has some real benefits for your career development. By seeking out opportunities to develop new skills in different parts of your organisation, you not only make yourself more valuable to your employer but also ensure that your value increases in the external employment market.

Whatever your reason for considering a lateral move, make sure that this contributes towards the achievement of your career goals and objectives.

Networking will help you to learn all you need to know about another area of the business. Begin by carrying out some research. Are there any internal reports or papers that would provide some information? Find out the names and titles of all the senior people in the new area and any others you consider might be of help to you. If you don't know any of these people personally, you'll have to create an opportunity to meet one of them. Phone one of the people on your list (not the most senior person) and ask for a short meeting. It's best to arrange this first meeting for outside normal working hours. Offer to buy them lunch, or perhaps arrange to have a drink in a local pub after office hours. Treat this as an informational meeting (see Chapter 4) and work at establishing a good relationship. Tell your contact that you have a genuine interest in their department and would be keen to hear more about the work that's carried out there. Make sure this meeting lasts no more than 30 minutes, as it's important not to outstay your welcome. Thank your contact and indicate that you'd like to keep in touch.

If the information you obtain is positive, tell your current manager that you'd like some background information about the new department and could you arrange a short meeting with their manager. Explain that you need this information for your personal development and not that you're considering a lateral move. It's too early at this stage to make any definite decisions. When you're sure that a move would be beneficial, tell your manager, since you don't want to be accused of disloyalty. Your meeting with the manager of the new department should also be conducted as an information meeting. Don't disclose that you're considering a lateral move until you've had an opportunity to carefully consider all the information.

Case Study

Lateral moves

Michael, a 28 year-old operations supervisor, was keen to make progress with his employer, a company in the security services industry. He'd discussed the lack of promotion opportunities with his immediate boss on several occasions and during his last appraisal meeting. The company recognised his potential but since it was a big step to the next job in his area of the business, and Michael's boss occupied this post, it was unlikely he'd be promoted to this job.

The company's human resource manager suggested that Michael should be moved on a lateral basis to a vacancy in sales administration for approximately 12 months. Following this, they anticipated transferring him to the field sales force for further development. At first, Michael wasn't happy with the proposal, but eventually he began to appreciate that this would add to his experience and would make him more marketable both inside and outside the company.

CUSTOMERS

You can also work on your career development by building relationships with customers. If you're not in sales, then opportunities for building relationships will be far fewer, but remember that it's in your interests to create opportunities.

When speaking to customers, the lesson you must quickly learn is that you're investing in a potentially long-term relationship. We know that successful relationships are built on a two-way flow of benefits and information – in other words, they're based on mutuality. Relationships with customers grow beyond the formal stage in a back and forth fashion. In order to move the relationship forward, either you or the customer must take a risk and disclose more about yourselves. Take a chance, and insert some small personal comment into an otherwise business conversation. If the response is positive, then you know the customer is in tune with you.

As with any other relationship in networking, try to find something that you have in common with your customers. People feel safer if they can do this, especially if you share the same values. Show an interest in what your customers say. Refer back to the section on communication in Chapter 3, and in particular refresh your memory about the importance of listening. Your aim should be to build relationships based on mutual respect and trust. When this has been achieved, it's quite likely that several of your customers may become friends as well as business contacts.

How then can networking with customers benefit your career development? Some of your customers will work for organisations that spend a lot of their profit on research and development. In such cases, you should be able to tap into this knowledge because of your relationship with the customer. Others may work for organisations that are prepared to try out the newest management theories. Again, you can pick up a great deal of helpful information before trying out the latest idea yourself.

If you're particularly good at dealing with customers, then you probably spend quite a lot of time with them. From this, you can discover what new products or services your customers need that your organisation can supply. You can also nip problems in the bud before they grow out of all proportion. It also allows you to establish very early on whether competitors are making in-roads into your territory.

If you've established a good relationship with your customer contacts, should they leave their current job, they'll probably tell their replacement about you. In this way, you should be able to maintain links with the old contact and be in an ideal position to establish a new one.

NETWORKING USING THE INTERNET

The Internet is one of the fastest ways of getting information. You can get up-to-the-minute news and talk to other people using e-mail or special interest bulletin boards. Most companies that use computers now use the Internet, but because it can be abused, they limit its use to certain people. If you're seriously interested in developing and managing your own career, talk to your employer about allowing you to access the Internet. The good news is that the costs are falling all the time. Certain Internet Service Providers, or ISPs, offer free access, whilst others charge a flat monthly fee. An ISP has computers called servers, which remain permanently connected to other computers on the Net via high-speed data links. All calls to your ISP are normally charged at local BT rate.

The Internet and World Wide Web are fast becoming important means of communication and research. Home pages are the latest way to present your qualifications and experience to the rest of the world. By its own estimates, the Web is growing at 1% per day: at that rate, there could be a home page for everyone in the world within four years.

To benefit from this technology, first you need to be computer literate. This may mean attending a training course at your local technical college, but it's well worth it. Second, sign up to the Internet. Once you're online, try exploring the resources available in your career area. Much of what you first see may be disappointing, uninteresting or irrelevant. However, given time and more intelligent search engines, this method of networking for career information will soon prove worthwhile.

Details of search engines and recruitment websites can be found in the resource directory at the end of this book.

REMEMBER

✔ To protect your career you must take responsibility for your continuing education and personal development.

✔ You must learn new skills and maintain an awareness of new developments in your chosen field.

✔ Ensure that the important people in your organisation recognise your transferable skills, achievements and career objectives.

✔ A mentor will contribute greatly to your continuing education and development and can be extremely valuable in introducing you to contacts in their own personal network.

✔ Achieving visibility within your organisation is an important part of self-marketing and career development.

✔ You can also work on your career development by building relationships with customers.

✔ Lateral moves are an important part of career development.

✔ With customers, your aim should be to build relationships based on mutual respect and trust.

✔ The Internet and World Wide Web are fast becoming important means of communication and research.

7 Conclusion

Adapting to change is key to keeping your career alive, provided you're prepared to take charge of your career and manage it yourself. This isn't an easy task and you'll need effective skills of your own and the help of appropriate and useful contacts to succeed. As a proven and reliable method of building a community of personal, social, business and professional contacts, networking is not simply desirable, but essential.

To network effectively you need a variety of skills and the ability to research. Combine these with self-esteem and personal motivation and you can build relationships that will ensure your career flourishes throughout your working life. Remember, too, that networking is not something you can put on a shelf only to bring down on suitable occasions; you must always be ready to network at a moment's notice.

Take good care of your contacts: they're too valuable to neglect. Always bear in mind that networking is about mutuality. If you only ever take from your contacts, then your relationships will suffer.

The end of this book marks the beginning of a long-term learning process. Putting into practice the advice and guidance outlined in these pages should help you on your journey.

In this guide you will find a list of transferable skills and a personal strengths and weaknesses inventory. When ranking your transferable skills **1** is your strongest asset.

LIST OF TRANSFERABLE SKILLS

People skills	Tick this box ✔ if this skill applies to you	Tick this box ✔ if this skill needs further development	Rank each of your skills
Advising – *Recommending a course of action.*			
Caring – *Having a strong concern for others.*			
Coaching – *Guiding the activities of others.*			
Communicating – *Conveying, receiving and sharing information.*			
Contacting – *Keeping in touch.*			
Counselling – *Helping people with personal, emotional and work problems.*			
Delegating – *Handing over tasks to subordinates. Briefing them correctly and monitoring their performance.*			
Encouraging – *Inspiring someone and instilling them with confidence.*			
Handling complaints – *Dealing with grievances, justified and unjustified, from staff and the public.*			
Influencing – *Persuading someone to alter or agree with a particular course of action.*			
Instructing – *Teaching. Making known to someone what you require him or her to do.*			

People skills *cont'd*	Tick this box ✔ if this skill applies to you	Tick this box ✔ if this skill needs further development	Rank each of your skills
Interviewing – Assessing someone's suitability for a job. Obtaining information using a questioning technique.			
Leading – Encouraging and inspiring individuals and teams to give their best to achieve a desired result.			
Listening – Gathering information whilst establishing rapport with the speaker.			
Managing – Deciding what to do and then getting it done through the effective use of people and other resources.			
Mediating – Bringing about a settlement, agreement or compromise between two or more parties. Acting as a liaison between competing interests.			
Negotiating – Setting objectives, deciding on strategy, and persuading and bargaining to get agreement and commitment.			
Organising – Getting things done in a well-ordered, efficient and methodical manner.			
Selling – Persuading someone to buy a product or service.			
Speaking in public – Communicating with an audience to motivate, inform or entertain.			
Supervising – Overseeing and inspecting work or workers.			
Training – Bringing a person or group of people to an agreed standard of proficiency by practice and instruction.			

Reasoning and judging skills	Tick this box ✔ if this skill applies to you	Tick this box ✔ if this skill needs further development	Rank each of your skills
Analysing – *Examining in detail to break down into components or essential features.*			
Appraising – *Evaluating programmes or services, judging the value of something, evaluating the performance of people.*			
Calculating – *Performing mathematical computations, assessing the risks of an activity.*			
Decision-making – *Choosing between priorities and options.*			
Designing – *Inventing, describing and depicting the parts or details of something according to a plan.*			
Editing – *Checking and improving the accuracy of documents.*			
Evaluating – *Judging or assessing the value of something.*			
General alternatives – *Producing a choice between two or more items or courses of action.*			
Innovating – *Creating and developing new ideas or solutions to problems.*			
Interpreting data – *Explaining or clarifying the meaning of facts or figures.*			
Investigating – *Analysing, evaluating and seeking new solutions.*			
Problem-solving – *Using reason to reach solutions.*			
Reviewing – *Examining to determine whether changes should be made.*			
Shaping – *Planning and moulding something into a desired form.*			
Validating – *Assuring the certainty of something in order to dispel any doubt.*			

Co-ordinating skills	Tick this box ✔ if this skill applies to you	Tick this box ✔ if this skill needs further development	Rank each of your skills
Administering – Taking charge of an area of work or tasks.			
Arranging – Making preparations and plans.			
Assembling – Gathering together a collection of parts.			
Constructing – Building or erecting together parts as a whole.			
Controlling – Comparing what's being achieved with what should have been achieved and, when appropriate, taking corrective action.			
Co-ordinating – Blending things together to achieve a desired result.			
Developing – Expanding or improving to an enhanced state.			
Driving – Operating and guiding a motor vehicle.			
Erecting – Raising or constructing (a building, for example).			
Fitting – Installing, connecting or attaching.			
Identifying priorities – Establishing the best order.			
Inspecting – Examining carefully and critically for flaws.			
Liaising – Contacting and communicating on a regular basis.			
Mechanical dexterity – Able to work with machinery.			
Monitoring – Observing and checking.			
Operating equipment – Being in charge of a working piece of equipment.			
Optimising – Making the most effective use of something.			
Planning – Formulating a programme for the achievement of an objective.			

Co-ordinating skills *cont'd*	Tick this box ✔ if this skill applies to you	Tick this box ✔ if this skill needs further development	Rank each of your skills
Predicting – *Forecasting outcomes.*			
Timing – *Organising time efficiently so that tasks are completed in a set period.*			
Trouble shooting – *Locating and eliminating sources of trouble.*			

Information skills	Tick this box ✔ if this skill applies to you	Tick this box ✔ if this skill needs further development	Rank each of your skills
Budgeting – *Outlining the cost of a project; assuring that spend will not exceed available funds; using money efficiently.*			
Classifying – *Arranging or organising according to class or category.*			
Clerical – *Describing skills used by those working in offices.*			
Compiling – *Gathering numerical, statistical data, accumulating facts about a given topic.*			
Computing – *Describing skills used by operators of high-tech equipment.*			
Corresponding with – *Communicating by letter.*			
Data-gathering – *Collecting information for analysis.*			
Diagnosing – *Investigating and determining the nature of a problem.*			
Dispensing information – *Giving out information in various formats.*			
Drafting reports – *Preparing provisional documents, the content of which are subject to approval before being released.*			
Fact-finding – *Discovering accurate information.*			
Information extraction – *Drawing out information.*			

Information skills cont'd	Tick this box ✔ if this skill applies to you	Tick this box ✔ if this skill needs further development	Rank each of your skills
Numerical – Working effectively with numbers.			
Observing – Watching carefully.			
Recording – Keeping an account of events or facts to serve as a source of information for the future.			
Researching – Investigating or enquiring in order to gather information about a subject. Physical observations.			
Surveying – Inspecting or examining in a comprehensive and detailed way the condition or quantity of a given subject.			
Updating – Keeping a file of information up to date. Completing records or acquiring new information on an old topic.			
Writing – Communicating using the written word.			

Originating skills	Tick this box ✔ if this skill applies to you	Tick this box ✔ if this skill needs further development	Rank each of your skills
Achieving – Successfully accomplishing something because of effort, skill or perseverance.			
Anticipating – Staying one step ahead. Being able to sense changes. Expecting it before it happens.			
Creating – Producing new ideas, plans and new ways of looking at things.			
Establishing – Creating and setting up something.			
Initiating – Beginning or introducing something.			
Promoting – Raising awareness in others of a subject's benefits.			
Responsibility-taking – Willingly taking control of something.			
Visualising – Being able to picture things in the mind.			

Personal strengths	Achievement rating		
	Small	**Moderate**	**Significant**
Able to maintain confidentiality			
Able to take risks			
Able to work under stress			
Accurate			
Adaptable			
Ambitious			
Assertive			
Caring			
Confident			
Conscientious			
Courageous			
Creative			
Decisive			
Dependable			
Diligent			
Diplomatic			
Enthusiastic			
Even-tempered			
Flexible			
Genuine			
Good under pressure			
Helpful			
Honest			
Imaginative			
Independent minded			

Personal strengths	Achievement rating		
	Small	Moderate	Significant
Intuitive			
Inventive			
Loyal			
Organised			
Original			
Outgoing			
Patient			
Perceptive			
Persistent			
Positive			
Practical			
Punctual			
Quick-thinking			
Rational			
Reliable			
Resilient			
Resourceful			
Responsible			
Self-disciplined			
Self-reliant			
Self-starting			
Shows initiative			
Sociable			
Spontaneous			
Strong work ethic			
Systematic			

Personal strengths	Achievement rating		
	Small	Moderate	Significant
Tactful			
Tenacious			
Thorough			
Thoughtful			
Tidy			
Tolerant			
Trustworthy			
Truthful			
Understanding			
Versatile			
Weaknesses			
Avoids confrontation			
Dogmatic			
Domineering			
Emotional			
Forthright			
Headstrong			
Impractical			
Impulsive			
Inconsiderate			
Inconsistent			
Indecisive			
Laid back			
Meddlesome			
Naïve			
Obsessive			

Personal weaknesses	Achievement rating		
	Small	**Moderate**	**Significant**
Obstinate			
Over-cautious			
Perfectionist			
Quarrelsome			
Reckless			
Self-opinionated			
Single-minded			
Too demanding of others			
Uninspiring			
Workaholic			

INTERNET RECRUITMENT

Search engines

www.excite.com
www.excite.co.uk
www.infoseek.com
www.lycos.com
www.lycos.co.uk
www.webcrawler.com
www.yahoo.com
www.yahoo.co.uk
www.god.co.uk
www.ukplus.co.uk

UK online recruitment websites

Top Jobs on the Net – Offers a range of general positions.
Contact: **www.topjobs.net**

The Appointments Section – Offers a range of IT and telecommunications jobs.
Contact: **www.taps.com**

The Monster Board – Offers a range of jobs.
Contact: **www.monster.co.uk**

Jobsunlimited – *The Guardian*'s site.
Contact: **www.jobsunlimited.co.uk**

The Language Site – Offers jobs for specialists in translation work.
Contact: **www.interscript.com/**

Jobmail – Offers jobs in IT, education, engineering and the legal sector.
Contact: **www.jobmail.co.uk**

Job Hunter – Updated daily by the UK's regional press.
Contact: **www.jobhunter.co.uk**

Jobs in Food – Offers all types of jobs in catering.
Contact: **www.cateringnet.co.uk**

Jobserve – Claims to be the largest source of IT vacancies in the UK.
Contact: **www.jobserve.com/**

Jobsite – Offers a range of vacancies.
Contact: **www.jobsite.co.uk**

Marketing Week – Offers marketing jobs and articles appearing in the magazine.
Contact: **www.marketingweek.co.uk/index.htm/**

Netjobs – Offers a range of vacancies.
Contact: **www.netjobs.co.uk**

Personnel Health – Specialises in healthcare jobs.
Contact: **www.personnelnet.com/**

Jobs in UK Journalism – Specialises in vacancies for journalists looking for work in magazines and newspapers in the UK and worldwide.
Contact: **www.journalism.co.uk**

Jobs Go Public – Specialises in jobs in the public sector, charity and voluntary sectors.
Contact: **www.jobsgopublic.com**

Prospects website – Association of Graduate Careers Advisory Services (AGCAS). For jobs and occupational information.
Contact: **www.prospects.csu.man.ac.uk**

NEWSPAPERS

National newspaper job advertisements		
Newspaper	**Day of the week**	**Job sector**
Daily Mail	Tuesday	Clerical
		Secretarial
	Thursday	Clerical
		Engineering
		General Appointments
		Overseas
		Printing & Publishing
		Retail
		Sales
		Technical
Daily Telegraph	Thursday	Executive/Management
		General Appointments
The European	Wednesday	General Appointments in the European Community
The Express	Thursday	Catering/Hotel
		Engineering
		General Appointments
		Sales
		Technical
Financial Times	Wednesday	Banking
		Finance
		General Appointments
	Thursday	Accountancy
		Finance
The Guardian	Monday	Creative & Media
		Fund-raising
		Marketing
		PR
		Sales
		Secretarial

National newspaper job advertisements		
Newspaper	**Day of the week**	**Job sector**
The Guardian	Tuesday	Education
		General Appointments
	Wednesday	Environment
		Health
		Housing
		Public Sector
	Saturday	Careers
		Creative & Media
		Education
		General Appointments
		Graduates
		IT
		Marketing
		PR
The Independent	Tuesday	Public Sector
	Wednesday	Sales
		Science
		IT
		Accounting
		Banking
		Clerical
	Thursday	Finance
		Legal
The Independent on Sunday	Sunday	Office
Mail on Sunday	Sunday	Multilingual
The Observer	Sunday	Secretarial
		Education
		Graduates
		General Appointments
		All Sectors
		IT
Scotsman	Monday	General Appointments
	Tuesday	General Appointments
	Wednesday	General Appointments
		Education
	Thursday	General Appointments
		Public Sector

National newspaper job advertisements		
Newspaper	**Day of the week**	**Job sector**
Scotsman	Friday	General Appointments Marketing Sales
Sunday Telegraph	Sunday	Repeat of Thursday's Appointments Supplement
The Sunday Times	Sunday	All Sectors
The Times	Wednesday	Secretarial
	Thursday	Management Senior Appointments Secretarial
	Friday	Education Marketing Media Sales

A SELECTION OF OTHER PUBLICATIONS CARRYING JOB ADVERTISEMENTS

Accountancy Age	Weekly
Architects' Journal	Weekly
Artists and Illustrators	Monthly
Banker, The	Monthly
British Journal of Photography	Weekly
British Medical Journal	Weekly
Building	Weekly
Caterer & Hotelkeeper	Weekly
Chemist & Druggist	Weekly
Community Care	Weekly
Education	Weekly
Engineering	Monthly
Farmers' Weekly	Weekly

Financial Advisor	Weekly
Grocer, The	Weekly
Housebuilder	Monthly
Insurance Age	Monthly
Lawyer, The	Weekly
Local Government Chronicle	Weekly
Marketing Week	Weekly
Media Week	Weekly
Money Marketing	Weekly
New Civil Engineer	Weekly
New Media Age	Weekly
Nursing Times & Nursing Mirror	Weekly
People Management	Bi-monthly
Printing World	Weekly
Retail Weekly	Weekly
Soap Perfumery & Cosmetics	Monthly
Sports Trader	Monthly
Surveyor	Weekly
Travel Trade Gazette	Weekly
Woodworker, The	Monthly

NETWORKING FOR WOMEN WEBSITE ADDRESSES

Women into Business (part of the Small Business Bureau). Contact: **www.smallbusinessbureau.org.uk/women/index.htm**

Network for Successful UK Women. Contact: **www.networkwomenuk.org/**

USEFUL ADDRESSES

Sources of career and industry information

Many of these organisations can provide you with useful career information or background to their industry. Send a letter setting out the information you require and for what purpose.

Administrative and clerical

Association of Medical Secretaries, Practice Administrators and Receptionists Ltd
Tavistock House North
Tavistock Square
London WC1H 9LN
Tel: 020 7387 6005

Advertising

The Advertising Association
Abford House
15 Wilton Road
London SW1V 1NJ
Tel: 020 7828 2771

Ambulance services

London Ambulance Service
The Recruitment Department
Central Division HQ
St Andrews House
St Andrews Way
Devons Road
London E3 3PA
Tel: 020 7887 6638

Animals

Animal Care College
Ascot House
29a High Street
Ascot
Berkshire SL5 7JG
Tel: 01344 628269

British Veterinary Nursing Association Ltd
Level 15
Terminus House
Terminus Street
Harlow
Essex CM20 IXA
Tel: 01279 450567

RSPCA
The Causeway
Horsham
West Sussex RH12 IHG
Tel: 0990 555999

Architecture
Architects and Surveying Institute
15 St Mary Street
Chippenham
Wiltshire SN15 3WD
Tel: 01249 444505

Art and design
Association of Illustrators
81 Leonard Street
London EC2A 4QS
Tel: 020 7613 4328

Chartered Society of Designers
1st Floor
32–38 Saffron Hill
London EC1N 8SG
Tel: 020 7831 9777

Banking
Chartered Institute of Bankers
4–9 Burgate Lane
Canterbury
Kent CT1 2XJ
Tel: 01227 762600

Beauty and hairdressing
Hairdressing and Beauty Industry Authority
Fraser House
Netherhall Road
Doncaster DN1 2PH
Tel: 01302 380000

National Hairdressers' Federation
11 Goldington Road
Bedford MK40 3JY
Tel: 01234 360332

Civil service
The Establishment Officer
Ordnance Survey
Romsey Road
Maybush
Southampton SO16 4GU
Tel: 02380 792000

Communications
Federation of Communications Services
Keswick House
207 Anerley Road
London SE20 8ER
Tel: 020 8778 5656

Computing
National Training Organisation for Information Technology
16–18 Berners Street
London W1P 3DD
Tel: 020 7580 6677

Construction
Construction Industry Training Board
Newton Training Centre
Bircham Newton
King's Lynn
Norfolk PE31 6RH
Tel: 01485 577577

Dentistry
British Dental Association
64 Wimpole Street
London WIM 8AL
Tel: 020 7935 0875

British Association of Dental Nurses
11 Pharos Street
Fleetwood
Lancashire FY7 6BG
Tel: 01253 778631

Engineering
Engineering Construction Industry Training Board
Blue Court
Church Lane
Kings Langley
Hertfordshire WD4 8JP
Tel: 01923 260000

The Engineering Careers Information Service
Enta House
14 Upton Road
Watford WD1 7EP
Tel: 0800 282167

Environment
Environment Agency
Public Enquiries Department
Rio House
Waterside Drive
Aztec West
Almondsbury
Bristol BS32 4UD
Tel: 01454 624400

English Nature
Enquiry Service
Room IE
Northminster House
Peterborough PEI IUA
Tel: 01733 455100

Finance
The Institute of Financial Accountants
Burford House
44 London Road
Sevenoaks
Kent TN13 IAS
Tel: 01732 458080

Chartered Institute of Management Accountants
63 Portland Place
London WIN 4AB
Tel: 020 7637 2311

Food and drink
Food and Drink National Training Organisation
Training Executive
6 Catherine Street
London WC2B 5JJ
Tel: 020 7836 2460

Gardening
Royal Horticultural Society
Supervisor of Studies and Training
Wisley
Woking
Surrey GU23 6QB
Tel: 01483 224234

The Institute of Horticulture
14–15 Belgrave Square
London SWIX 8PS
Tel: 020 7245 6943

Health service
NHS Careers
PO Box 376
Bristol BS99 3EY
Tel: 0845 6060655

Hotel and catering
Hotel, Catering and International Management Association
191 Trinity Road
London SW17 7HN
Tel: 020 8672 4251

Human resources and personnel
Institute of Personnel and Development
Camp Road
Wimbledon
London SW19 4UX
Tel: 020 8971 9000

Insurance
The Chartered Insurance Institute
20 Aldermanbury
London EC2V 7HY
Tel: 020 7417 4793

Languages
The Institute of Linguists
Saxon House
48 Southwark Street
London SE1 1UN
Tel: 020 7940 3100

Law
The Law Society
Legal Education Information Unit
Ipsley Court
Berrington Close
Redditch
Worcestershire B98 0TD
Tel: 01527 517141

Institute of Legal Executives
Kempston Manor
Kempston
Bedfordshire MK42 7AB
Tel: 01234 841000

Crown Prosecution Service
Recruitment Branch
50 Ludgate Hill
London EC4M 7EX
Tel: 020 7796 8000

Library work
The Library Association
7 Ridgmount Street
London WC1E 7AE
Tel: 020 7255 0500

Management
Institute of Management
Management House
Cottingham Road
Corby
Northants NN17 1TT
Tel: 01536 204222

Marketing
The Chartered Institute of Marketing
Moor Hall
Cookham
Maidenhead
Berkshire SL6 9QH
Tel: 01628 427310

Market research
The Market Research Society
15 Northburgh Street
London EC1V 0JR
Tel: 020 7490 4911

The media
National Council for the Training of Journalists
The Latton Bush Centre
Southern Way
Harlow
Essex CM18 7BL
Tel: 01279 430009

Medical and nursing
British Medical Association
BMA House
Tavistock Square
London WC1H 9JP
Tel: 020 7387 4499

Royal College of Nursing
20 Cavendish Square
London W1M 0AB
Tel: 020 7409 3333

Pharmacy
The Royal Pharmaceutical Society of Great Britain
1 Lambeth High Street
London SE1 7JN
Tel: 020 7735 9141

Photography
Association of Photographers
31 Leonard Street
London EC2A 4QS
Tel: 020 7739 6669

Physiotherapy
The Chartered Society of Physiotherapy
14 Bedford Row
London WC1R 4ED
Tel: 020 7306 6666

Publishing and bookselling
The Publishers Association
1 Kingsway
London WC2B 6X0
Tel: 020 7565 7474

Booksellers Association of Great Britain
272 Vauxhall Bridge Road
London SW1V 1BA
Tel: 020 7834 5477

Sport
Sport England
16 Upper Woburn Place
London WC1H 0QP
Tel: 020 7273 1500

Sports Council for Northern Ireland
House of Sport
Upper Malone Road
Belfast BT9 5LA
Tel: 02890 381222

Sport Scotland
Caledonia House
South Gyle
Edinburgh EH12 9DQ
Tel: 0131 317 7200

The Sports Council for Wales
Sophia Gardens
Cardiff CF11 9SW
Tel: 029 2030 0500

Teaching
Teaching Training Agency
Portland House
Stag Place
London SW1E 5TT
Tel: 020 7925 3700

Travel and tourism
Institute of Travel and Tourism
113 Victoria Street
St Albans
Hertfordshire AL1 3TJ
Tel: 01727 854395

Interim management
Albemarle Interim Management Services
26–28 Great Portland Street
London W1N 5AD
Tel: 020 7631 1991

Ernst & Young Corporate Resources
Roll House
7 Rolls Buildings
Fetter Lane
London EC4A 1NH
Tel: 020 7951 2000

Executive Interim Management
39 St James' Street
London SW1A 1JD
Tel: 020 7290 1430

PA Consulting Group
123 Buckingham Palace Road
London SW1W 9SR
Tel: 020 7730 9000

Russam GMS Ltd
48 High Street North
Dunstable
Bedfordshire LU6 1LA
Tel: 01582 666970

Training and education

Information and advice can be obtained from the following:

Career Development Loans
Freepost
PO Box 354
Warrington WA4 6XU
Tel: 0800 585505

ECCTIS 2000
Oriel House
Oriel Road
Cheltenham
Gloucestershire GL50 1XP
Tel: 01242 252627

The Industrial Society
Robert Hyde House
48 Bryanston Square
London W1H 2EA
Tel: 020 7479 2000

Institute of Management
Management House
Cottingham Road
Corby
Northants NN17 1TT
Tel: 01536 204222

Institute of Personnel and Development
35 Camp Road
Wimbledon
London SW19 4UX
Tel: 020 8971 9000

Local Education Authorities (look in your local *Yellow Pages*)

National Extension College
18 Brooklands Avenue
Cambridge
CB2 2HN
Tel: 01223 450200

Open University
Admissions Office
PO Box 46
Milton Keynes MK7 6AP
Tel: 01908 274066

Royal Society of Arts
6 John Adam Street
London WC2N 6EZ
Tel: 020 7930 5115

FURTHER READING

Headhunters and recruitment consultants

The Executive Grapevine, published by Executive Grapevine International.

CEPEC Recruitment Guide, published by CEPEC Ltd.

The Personnel Manager's Yearbook, published by A. P. Information Services.

Yearbook of Recruitment and Employment Services, published by A. P. Information Services.

Public speaking

Suzy Siddon, *Presentation Skills*, Institute of Personnel and Development, September 1999.

Rosemary Riley, *A Straightforward Guide to Public Speaking*, Straightforward Publications, July 1997.

Christina Stuart, *Be an Effective Speaker*, National Textbook Company, January 1999.

Roger Mason, *Teach Yourself Speaking at Special Occasions*, Teach Yourself Books, November 1995.

John Bowden, *Making Effective Speeches*, How To Books, October 1998.

CAREER PUBLICATIONS FROM THE INDUSTRIAL SOCIETY

The Insider Guides

Job Search
Brian Sutton
ISBN 1 85835 815 9

Career Networking
Brian Sutton
ISBN 1 85835 825 6

Interviews & Assessments
Brian Sutton
ISBN 1 85835 820 5

The Insider Career Guides

Advertising, Marketing & PR
Karen Holmes
ISBN 1 85835 872 8

Banking & the City
Karen Holmes
ISBN 1 85835 583 4

Broadcasting & the Media
Paul Redstone
ISBN 1 85835 867 1

The Environment
Melanie Allen
ISBN 1 85835 588 5

Information & Communications Technology
Jacquetta Megarry
ISBN 1 85835 593 1

Retailing
Liz Edwards
ISBN 1 85835 578 8

Sport
Robin Hardwick
ISBN 1 85835 573 7

Travel & Tourism
Karen France
ISBN 1 85835 598 2